Fast & Fresh

MEDITERRANEAN

Fast & Fresh
MEDITERRANEAN

Delicious recipes to make in under 30 minutes

ODED SCHWARTZ

KYLE CATHIE LIMITED

First published in Great Britain in 1995 by
Kyle Cathie Limited
7/8 Hatherley Street
London SW1P 2QT

ISBN 1 85626 172 7

A Cataloguing in Publication record for this title is
available from the British Library.

Food stylist: Oded Schwartz
Design: Tamasin Cole
Printed and bound by Kyodo, Singapore.

Acknowledgements
This book would not have been possible without the help of the food
conveyors of Finchley: Gary and his crew at Ellinghams, Andi at Ellenas,
Pedro at P.S.Fisheries and Graham and David at Graham's Butchers. I am
grateful to them. And to Kyle who, although she never answers phone
calls, gives me the free hand and inspiration which are necessary for
creative writing. Finally, thanks to my photographer, Julie Dixon, who
is game for anything.
Thanks to the Kasbah, Southampton Row, and to Selfridges for the loan of props.

Contents

Introduction   6

Sauces & Stocks   8

Soups   20

Starters   30

Salads   44

Meat   56

Fish   72

Desserts   84

Index   95

Introduction

To many people, Mediterranean food is associated with memories of holidays in the sun, warm days spent in quayside cafés in Sicily and brilliant crimson evenings in a Greek or Turkish taverna and romantic beach trips in the South of France. But Mediterranean food is much more than that: it is a way of life. Religions, cultures and politics may differ but all around the shores of the Mediterranean people share more or less the same palate, share a way of life and use the same wonderful ingredients. They love to eat, drink, love and argue but, above all, entertain and be entertained.

In comparison with the size of the Mediterranean sea, the coast line covers very diverse areas – Spain, France, Italy, Yugoslavia, Albania, Greece and Turkey to the northern shore, Lebanon and Israel at the eastern end and Egypt, Libya, Tunisia and Morocco to the south. To the locals, the Mediterranean is affectionately known as the big pond. Indeed like a pond, it is a rich brew of cultures, peoples and influences. Western culture was born around the Mediterranean, Pharaohs ruled, the Bible was written, Greeks Hellenised, Roman Emperors conquered, Jesus was born and European Crusaders fought. And, when Europe was paralysed by the ravages of the Middle Ages, Arab and Ottoman warriors and merchants spread their influence all over the Mediterranean basin. They brought with them new knowledge and science, as well as new ingredients, spices from the East and cooking techniques that changed Europe forever.

Arab and Ottoman influences are especially noticed in the kitchen. Croissants, jam, pasta, marzipan, lemons, aubergines, spices and many more were either introduced or reintroduced into Europe in the wake of Islam.

Mediterranean food is robust. It is extremely tasty and very healthy. The diet is based on the Holy Trinity of wheat, pulses and olive oil, with the addition of a vast variety of vegetables, fruit and fish; thus it contains all the elements required for healthy living. In moderation, the fourth element of this trinity is the grape, adding both to health and, certainly, to the conviviality of life.

Cooking Mediterranean food is a lot of fun, and the fun starts with the shopping. Markets are a riot of colours, shapes, smells and noises. They are the place to meet friends, to gossip and exchange recipes, discuss ailments and remedies, and to flirt. Sadly not all of us live around this wonderful sea and have to welcome the rising popularity of Mediterranean cooking, with specialised ingredients now being sold by many supermarket chains.

Researching and writing this book gave me, a Mediterranean in exile, the opportunity to take a closer look at the basics of the cuisine I love. Although in each country the balance of flavour is unique, similar techniques reappear, ingredients are used in the same combinations and identical sauces crop up under different names.

While collecting the recipes, I came across one that, for me, crystallised the exact idea I started with – it was a recipe given to me by a Maltese lady, boasting French and Italian ancestry, and now married to a Turk. Basically this, in the kitchen at least, is what Mediterranean life is all about – a happy and delicious brew of cultures, traditions and above all, fun and flavour. Enjoy cooking!

Unless stated otherwise, the quantities given in these recipes are for 4 people.

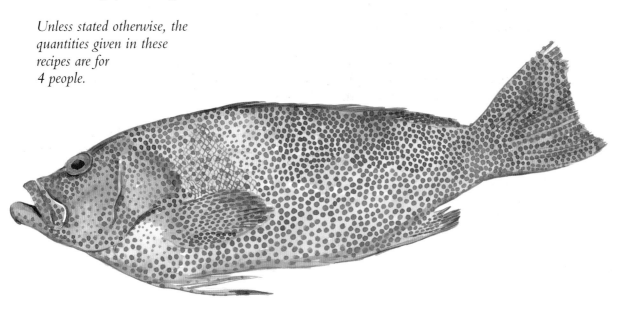

SAUCES

TAHINA SAUCE

Tahina is an essential ingredient of the eastern Mediterranean kitchen. The nutty flavour of sesame seeds goes well with fish and can be widely used in salads, pilavs and as a dip with raw vegetables.

juice of 2 or more lemons
250 g/8 oz/1 cup raw tahina paste
about 175 ml/6 fl.oz/3/4 cup water
1-2 cloves of garlic, mashed with a little salt
1 tablespoon parsley, finely chopped

1   Add the lemon juice to the tahina paste and mix well. To start with the tahina paste seems to separate and turns into a lumpy, grainy mass. Keep mixing, adding small quantities of water until the sauce reaches the right consistency. Add salt, garlic and parsley.

NOTE   When eaten as a dip tahina should be the consistency of a thick cream. For cooking however it needs to be thinner – like single cream. Dilute to the right consistency with lemon juice, water or milk.

HARISSA

This piquant and hot sauce is one of the most important flavourings of the north African kitchen. It is used to give fire to many dishes. I use it to flavour mayonnaise, yogurt, cheese, pasta, rice or just mixed with butter and spread onto fresh bread. There are hundreds of recipes for harissa; some are mild, some fiery and some bordering on deadly! This one is hot – but not deadly.

The heat of the sauce is dictated by the heat of the chillies, which vary greatly. For my harissa I use a combination of the large, not hot, red chillies (Westlands) and the very hot, small red chillies.

Use the harissa with discretion: first try adding one teaspoon and then progress until you reach a tolerable heat.

The quantity below makes about 500 g/1 lb/2 cups, which seems a lot but the sauce will keep for up to 3 months, covered, in the fridge.

150 g/6 oz/3/4 cup fresh red chillies (see above)
150 g/6 oz/2/3 cup tomatoes, peeled & de-seeded
3 tablespoons tomato purée
7 large cloves of garlic, peeled
1 teaspoon ground cumin
50 ml/2 fl. oz/1/4 cup vinegar
75 g/3 oz/1/3 cup olive oil
1 1/2 teaspoons salt

1   Remove the hard stems and de-seed the chillies. (For a hotter harissa, include the seeds.) Mince or process the chillies, tomatoes, tomato purée and garlic while adding the vinegar, oil and flavouring. Be careful to wash your hands very well after dealing with chillies.

2   Bottle in a glass jar. Cover with a thin layer of oil to prevent drying and seal tightly. The paste can be stored in the fridge for up to 3 months.

Harissa and
Salsa Verde (see page 12)

ROUGH TOMATO SAUCE

It is difficult to imagine the Mediterranean kitchen without tomatoes, considering that in many places the common use of the tomato started as late as the beginning of this century.

There is nothing more delicious then a local Mediterranean tomato, be they the fleshy Italian plum tomatoes that are essential for a good, full-bodied sauce or the slightly minty, sweet, big tomatoes sold in every local market. The tart sweetness of the tomato makes an ideal combination with olive oil, garlic and onion thus making the tomato the base for many sauces. The following are two versions of tomato sauce: the first a rough, mild sauce that goes very well with pasta or meat balls; the second, a smooth, spicy sauce that goes well with fish or chicken. Made thick enough, these sauces can be used as dips.

5 tablespoons virgin olive oil
2 medium onions, peeled & roughly chopped
3-4 fat cloves of garlic, peeled & roughly chopped
3 celery stems, finely chopped
1 kg/2 lb/4 cups Italian plum tomatoes, peeled, de-seeded & roughly chopped
1 tablespoon tomato purée
a large bouquet garni composed of a few twigs of thyme or oregano,
*   flat parsley, celery leaves & a strip or two of orange zest*
salt & freshly ground black pepper

1 Heat the oil in a heavy bottomed frying pan, add the onion, garlic and celery and fry, over high heat, stirring until the onion starts to change colour.

2 Add the rest of the ingredients and fry for a few minutes mixing all the time. Reduce the heat to minimum and simmer, uncovered for about 15 minutes; stir frequently to avoid scorching. If you prefer a smoother sauce, remove the bouquet garni, transfer into a food processor and process until smooth.

SPICY TOMATO SAUCE

4 tablespoons virgin olive oil
2 medium onions, peeled & roughly chopped
3-4 fat cloves of garlic, peeled & crushed
1-2 or more red chillies or ½ teaspoon or more good chilli powder (to taste)
1 fennel bulb, outer leaves discarded, chopped
1 scant teaspoon fennel seeds
1 kg/2 lb/4 cups Italian plum tomatoes, peeled, de-seeded & roughly chopped
1 tablespoon tomato purée
4 anchovy fillets, roughly chopped
salt & freshly ground black pepper

1   Heat the oil in a heavy bottomed frying pan, add the onion, garlic, chilli, fennel and fennel seeds. Fry for a few minutes, stirring, until the onion starts to be transparent. Add the tomatoes, the purée and the anchovy and continue to fry, over high heat, for a minute or two. Season to taste. Reduce the heat to minimum and simmer, uncovered, for 15 minutes.

2   Transfer the cooked mixture to a processor and process at high speed until the required texture is achieved. Return to the frying pan and re-heat. The sauce can be kept in the fridge, covered, for up to a week.

NOTE   To de-seed tomatoes, cut peeled tomatoes in half and squeeze out the seeds.

SALSA VERDE

This bright green and pungent sauce appears all over the Mediterranean. It is delicious served with grilled fish or grilled chicken. Serve it as a dressing on potato salad or just poured over burgul or rice as a light main course.

50 g/2 oz/¼ cup crustless white bread, soaked in water
1 large bunch of flat-leaf parsley, stems removed
75 g/3 oz/⅓ cup sorrel or spinach, washed well
25 g/1 oz/1½ tablespoons capers
50 g/2 oz/¼ cup anchovy fillet
1 hard boiled egg
2 tablespoons white wine vinegar
100 ml/4 fl.oz/½ cup olive oil

1 Squeeze the bread dry and put it together with the rest of the ingredients, except the oil, into a food processor. Process into a smooth cream.

2 With the machine running, add the oil in a slow, steady stream, like making mayonnaise. Process for a few seconds until the sauce is smooth and creamy. Refrigerate covered, until required.

GARLIC SAUCE

Garlic is one of the basic ingredients in the Mediterranean kitchen. The flavour of garlic changes as it cooks. Fresh garlic is pungent and hot in flavour while stewed garlic has an elusive, delicate perfume and has an exquisite melt-in-the-mouth texture. A sweet garlic preserve is often made in southern Italy. The sauce below belongs to a vast family of garlic sauces and is a bit less oily and therefore healthier than the French Aïoli. It is delicious served as a dip for fresh vegetables or to accompany grilled fish or meat.

The use of bread instead of egg yolks as an emulsifying agent is ancient. Soaked bread absorbs oil and makes a sauce with a texture similar to mayonnaise. This simple technique is especially important in a cholesterol-free diet. I like to include some fresh herbs in the sauce which add a lot of lightness to the intense garlic flavour.

100 g/4 oz/¹/2 cup good white bread, crust removed, soaked in water
1 head of garlic (about 6-8 cloves), peeled
juice of 1 lemon
grated zest of ¹/2 lemon
250 ml/8 fl.oz/1 cup olive oil
2 tablespoons chopped parsley (optional)

1 Squeeze the bread dry and put it into a food processor, together with all the other ingredients except the olive oil.

2 Process to a smooth cream. Add the oil in a thin steady stream while the machine is running, like making mayonnaise. The sauce can be kept for up to a week, in the fridge, in a tightly covered container.

TAPENADE

This delicious sauce encapsulates the flavour of the Mediterranean. Its origin is in the South of France and its name comes from the old Provençal word for capers – tapeno. Traditionally the sauce is made with a pestle and mortar which does not take much time but it involves experience and much elbow grease. Making it in the processor will take about 2 minutes but the texture is much too fine.

Most of the available stoned olives are, at best, tasteless. Therefore do buy good olives which, unfortunately, usually come with the stone. Stoning olives can be made easy with a special olive stoner. These are readily available in many kitchen equipment stores.

Tapenade is a versatile sauce. It is served as a dip with raw vegetables, as a spread on crusty bread or try it together with plenty of fresh herbs as a quick sauce for pasta. It keeps in the fridge for up to a month.

2 heaped tablespoons capers, drained
1 x 50 g/2 oz/¼ cup tin of anchovies, drained
250 g/8 oz/1 cup good black olives, stoned
4 tablespoons virgin olive oil
a few drops of lemon juice

1   Either put the capers and anchovies into a pestle and pound into a paste. Then add the olives a few at the time and pound until completely crushed. Add the olive oil, a little at a time, like making mayonnaise and pound until all the oil is absorbed and the mixture is homogenous. Add the lemon juice and mix well. Or, put the first 3 ingredients into the processor and process for 1 minute. While the machine is running add the oil in a thin steady stream, add the lemon juice and mix well. Cover and refrigerate.

NOTE   The anchovy marinating oil, especially if it is olive oil, can be added to the sauce. Remember to reduce the total quantity of oil accordingly.

AVGOLEMONO

Avgolemono is an egg and lemon sauce, an extremely versatile one suitable for fish, poultry and many vegetables such as plainly boiled asparagus, courgettes and globe artichokes. It is especially good with boiled chicken. The sauce, which is basically a savoury custard, is easy to make but be very careful not to overheat as the sauce, like any egg custard, can curdle easily.

4 egg yolks
100 ml/4 fl. oz/½ cup lemon juice (or to taste)
½ teaspoon grated lemon zest
250 ml/8 fl. oz/1 cup hot chicken stock
salt

1   Whisk the yolks until pale and frothy (about 2 minutes in a mixer at high speed). Add the lemon juice and zest and mix well. Whisk in the hot stock.

2   Transfer the mixture into the top of a double boiler, reduce the heat to minimum, and cook mixing all the time for about 4–5 minutes or until the sauce is just thick enough to coat a spoon. The sauce can be served either hot or cold.

SALSA AGRO-DOLCE

This sweet and sour sauce originated in the kitchens of the Roman Empire and is still used today all over the Mediterranean. It can be served instead of the traditional gravy with roast lamb or venison and makes an interesting base for meat balls or chicken ragù.

2 medium onions, peeled
2 tablespoons pine nuts
4 tablespoons olive oil
250 ml/8 fl. oz/1 cup chicken stock
2 tablespoons honey
100 g/4 oz/½ cup seedless raisins
1 tablespoon cornflour
4 tablespoons good red wine or sherry vinegar
salt
2 tablespoons chopped mint (optional)

1 Place the onion and pine nuts in the food processor and process at high speed until the mixture is chopped but not puréed.

2 Heat the oil in a heavy bottomed frying pan. Add the onion and nut mixture and fry for about 5 minutes or until nicely golden. Add the stock, honey and raisins. Reduce the heat and simmer gently for 10 minutes.

3 Dissolve the cornflour in the vinegar and add to the cooking sauce and simmer for a few minutes more. Add the salt and mint and serve hot, with cold meats or hot, roasted lamb or venison.

To use as cooking sauce: bring the sauce to simmering point and add the meat; continue to simmer for about 25-30 minutes or until meat is cooked.

FISH STOCK

Fish stock gives soups and stews much of their richness and individuality. The short time required to cook the fish is not enough for the gravy to develop depth of flavour. Making fish stock is quick and easy and the stock can be kept covered in the fridge for up to a week. It can be successfully frozen and kept for up to 3 months.

When buying fish ask also for extra skin and bones; most good fishmongers will gladly oblige. Try to avoid using the skins or bones of oily fish such as mackerel; white fish, trout and salmon make a good well balanced stock. I like my stock flavoursome; therefore I always include a red mullet with the fish head and bones which impart a delicious gamey aroma to the stock.

1 kg / 2 lb / 4 cups fish skin & bones
1 small red mullet (optional)
1 large onion, peeled & sliced
2 carrots, washed & sliced
1 fennel, washed & sliced
Bouquet garni made of a few stems & leaves of parsley & celery, a small sprig of thyme,
    a strip of lemon zest & 1-2 bay leaves
½ teaspoon black peppercorns
½ teaspoons fennel seeds (optional)
water to cover (or a mixture of water & white wine)

1   Wash the fish heads, bones and skin in a few changes of cold water and lay them on the bottom of a large, heavy bottomed pot.

2   Add the rest of the ingredients and cover with cold water. Bring to the boil, reduce the heat and simmer, very gently, for 20-25 minutes. Strain the liquid and use as needed.

QUICK CHICKEN STOCK

You probably wonder what a recipe for chicken stock is doing in a book which deals with fast food. The reason is that especially in fast cooking stock is an essential ingredient. It gives soups, sauces and stews the depth of flavour and texture which normally take long and slow cooking to achieve.

Making stock properly, although not technically complicated, takes a long time – with the help of a pressure cooker the cooking process takes only 20-25 minutes. Although not as clear or as refined, pressure cooking produces stock that can give body to otherwise thin and anaemic dishes. For extra body condense the stock by boiling it rapidly until reduced by half or even more. Fresh stock will last, covered, in the fridge for up to 2 weeks. It can also be frozen successfully for up to 3 months.

1 medium chicken (about 1¹/₂ kg/3 lb), cut into portions
2 large carrots, washed & coarsely chopped
1 large unpeeled onion, washed well & roughly sliced
3 celery sticks, roughly chopped
2 small tomatoes, halved
100 g/4 oz/¹/₂ cup of pumpkin or 1-2 courgettes
A bouquet garni made with a few sprigs of thyme, parsley, 2 bay leaves
*   & a small strip of lemon or orange peel*
4 cloves
¹/₂ teaspoon peppercorns
2.5 cm/1 in piece of cinnamon stick (optional)
water to cover (about 1.5 litres/3 pints/6 cups)

1   Place all the above ingredients in the pressure cooker. Cover with water, being careful not to exceed the manufacturer's recommendation. Cover tightly and bring to pressure (15 lb gauge). Reduce the heat and simmer, under pressure, for 20 minutes.

2   Remove the cooker from the heat and reduce the pressure under cold water. Strain the liquid. The stock can be used as required.

NOTE   The cooked chicken meat, mixed with potatoes and other cooked vegetables and served with garlic sauce (see page 13), makes an interesting salad.

AUBERGINE SOUP

Aubergines are not normally associated with soups but do try this recipe. It makes a delightfully piquant, pale pink soup. Serve with chunks of fresh bread and butter.

2 medium aubergines
3 tablespoons virgin olive oil
1 large onion, peeled & finely chopped
3 cloves of garlic, peeled and chopped
3 medium tomatoes, peeled, de-seeded & finely chopped
2 teaspoons tomato purée
1 litre / 2 pints / 4 cups chicken stock
2 tablespoons lemon juice
salt & freshly ground black pepper
4 tablespoons basil leaves, roughly chopped

1 Heat oven to maximum 250°C/475°F/Gas Mark 9. With a fork, prick the aubergines in a few places and bake them for about 15-20 minutes or until very soft.

2 Heat the oil in a heavy bottomed pan, add the onion and garlic and fry over high heat for a few minutes or until the onion starts to change colour. Add the tomatoes, tomato purée, stock and lemon juice and bring to the boil. Reduce the heat and simmer for a few minutes.

3 When the aubergines are ready, remove from the oven, cut them in halves and scoop out the flesh carefully (they are very hot). Place in a food processor and process into a smooth purée.

4 Add the purée to the simmering soup and continue to simmer for a minute or two. Season with salt and pepper to taste. Add the basil and serve hot.
   A tablespoon of thick cream could be stirred in just before serving.

COLD ALMOND SOUP

The following soup is a direct descendent of a medieval Spanish recipe, and surprisingly makes a delicious and different summer soup. I tried it once with roasted almonds, and although the flavour was superb, the beige colour of the soup put people off. I sometimes add a few drops of natural bitter almond essence to intensify the almond flavour.

150 g / 6 oz / ³/4 cup almonds, blanched and peeled
100 g / 4 oz / ¹/2 cup bread, crustless, soaked in cold water
2 cloves of garlic
6 ice cubes
4 tablespoons good olive oil
juice of 1 lemon
salt
500 ml / 1 pint / 2 cups very cold chicken stock or water
100 g / 4 oz / ¹/2 cup cucumber, chopped
100 g / 4 oz / ¹/2 cup apple, chopped
4 sprigs of mint

1 Place the almonds in the food processor and process, at high speed, until the almonds are powdered. Squeeze the bread to exude as much moisture as possible and add to the almonds together with the garlic, ice cubes, lemon juice, zest and salt and process to a smooth cream.

2 With the machine still running, gradually add the oil. Transfer the mixture into a large serving bowl, add the stock and mix well. Adjust the seasoning and serve, very cold, decorated with some of the chopped apples and cucumber and a sprig of mint. The rest of the chopped cucumber and apple is sent to the table separately so diners can help themselves.

PUMPKIN & TOMATO SOUP

A colourful and savoury autumn soup that can be served either as it is or creamed.

3 tablespoons olive oil
500 g / 1 lb / 2 cups pumpkin, peeled & cubed
3 large tomatoes, peeled, de-seeded & chopped
1 large onion, peeled & finely chopped
2 green chillies, de-seeded & chopped (or more to taste)
1 litre / 2 pints / 4 cups water or stock
1 teaspoon freshly ground coriander
salt
a few coriander leaves for decoration

1 Heat the oil in a large, heavy bottomed pan. Add all the vegetables and the ground coriander and fry over medium heat for about 5 minutes. Stir from time to time to mix and prevent scorching.

2 Add the liquid and bring to the boil. Skim, reduce the heat and simmer gently for about 20 minutes. Add the salt, sprinkle with coriander leaves and serve hot.

3 If you prefer a smooth finish, strain the soup and return the liquid to the cooking pot. Transfer the vegetables into a food processor and process, at high speed, into a smooth purée. Return to the pot, heat through and finish as above.

WINTER TOMATO SOUP

A satisfying and warming winter soup. Served with a chunk of bread and cheese, it makes a warming lunch dish.

3 tablespoons olive oil
1 teaspoon whole cumin
100 g / 4 oz / ½ cup onion, chopped
3 cloves of garlic, peeled
1 kg / 2 lb Italian tomatoes, sliced into large chunks
250 ml / 8 fl.oz / 1 cup water
100 g / 4 oz / ½ cup fresh breadcrumbs
juice of 1 orange
1 tablespoon chopped flat-leaf parsley or basil
salt & freshly ground black pepper

1 Heat the oil in a large, heavy bottomed pan. Add the cumin and fry for 2 minutes or until the cumin starts to pop and emits a pleasant roasted smell. Add the onion and garlic and fry until the onion starts to change colour. Add the tomatoes and the water and simmer for about 5 minutes.

2 Transfer to a food processor and process until smooth. Sieve the mixture into a clean pan, season with salt and pepper, add the orange juice and breadcrumbs and bring to the boil. Reduce the heat and simmer for about 10 minutes. Serve hot, sprinkled with chopped parsley or basil.

OKRA SOUP

Okra is a versatile vegetable with a wonderful earthy flavour and an interesting texture.. Cooked one way it supplies a smooth, almost velvety finish to soups and stews, cooked another it can be served as a deliciously crunchy salad. Okra is available almost all year round in Greek, Mediterranean and Indian grocers. It is also available in some supermarkets.

Select young, fresh, intensely green pods the ends of which should snap off crisply. Avoid yellowed limp pods that are tough and stringy. To prepare the okra remove the hard stem and wash well.

4 tablespoons virgin olive oil
150 g/6 oz/³/4 cup leek, finely chopped
2 medium tomatoes, peeled, de-seeded & chopped
1 tablespoon tomato purée
1 litre/2 pints/4 cups chicken or vegetable stock
250 g/8 oz/1 cup young okra, trimmed & sliced into 2.5 cm/1 in slices
2 tablespoons lemon juice
salt
chopped parsley

1 Heat 2 tablespoons of the oil in a large, heavy bottomed pan and add the okra. Fry over a high heat until the okra starts to brown. Lift out the okra and drain on absorbent kitchen roll.

2 Heat the rest of the oil. Add the leeks and fry, over high heat, for a minute or two or until the leek becomes transparent. Stir in the tomatoes, tomato purée and the stock and bring to the boil. Reduce the heat and simmer for 10 minutes or until the okra is tender.

3 Season with lemon and salt just before serving. Serve hot decorated with chopped parsley.

GARLIC SOUP

The recipe is a version of the Provençal *soupe au pistou* – **a must for garlic lovers! This robust soup is from the African coast of the Mediterranean where it acquired its pungency. The amount of harissa below will give a pleasant hottish glow. Watch the frying garlic very closely as it tends to burn easily.**

2 tablespoons olive oil
1 large head of garlic, peeled & roughly chopped
3 medium potatoes, peeled & coarsely grated
3 medium tomatoes, peeled, de-seeded & coarsely grated
500 g/1 lb/2 cups French beans, sliced into 2.5 cm/1 in lengths
1 litre/2 pints/4 cups water or stock
75 g/3 oz/⅓ cup vermicelli
salt & freshly ground black pepper

for the sauce
4 cloves of garlic, peeled
50 g/2 oz/¼ cup basil leaves
1 large tomato, peeled & de-seeded
1 tablespoon harissa or more (see page 9)
4 tablespoons of the soup

1　Heat the oil in a heavy bottomed pan, add the garlic and fry for 1 minute or until the garlic just starts to change colour. Add the potatoes, tomatoes and the beans, together with the liquid, and bring to the boil. Reduce the heat and simmer for 15 minutes. Add the vermicelli and the seasoning and cook for a further 5-8 minutes or until all is just tender.

2　To make the sauce put all the ingredients into a food processor and process into a smooth cream.

3　Stir the sauce into the soup, mix well and transfer into a heated tureen.

WHITE FOAM SOUP

This curious Spanish soup has an extraordinary texture, that of a very soft and velvety cheese soufflé. Use a good mature cheese such as hard mountain Spanish or cheddar.

25 g/1 oz/1½ tablespoons butter
1 onion, peeled & chopped
2 cloves of garlic, peeled & crushed
1 stick celery, chopped
½ tablespoon flour
1 litre/2 pints/4 cups milk
1 blade of mace (or ½ a nutmeg)
2 eggs
50 g/2 oz/¼ cup grated cheese
salt & freshly ground black pepper
1 tablespoon chopped parsley
4 tablespoons garlic croûtons

1   Melt the butter in a heavy bottomed pan, add the onion, garlic and celery and fry for a few moments.

2   Sprinkle with the flour and continue to fry for a minute or two. Add the milk and the mace, bring to the boil, reduce the heat and simmer for 15 minutes.

3   In the meantime separate the eggs and beat the whites into a stiff snow.

4   Remove the pot from the heat and allow to cool for a minute or two. Beat the yolks and add to the pot together with the cheese. Mix well and fold in half the egg white. Return to the heat and re-heat, being careful never to let the soup boil.

5   Transfer the rest of the egg white to a heated soup tureen and pour over the hot soup. Serve immediately, sprinkled with chopped parsley and well-flavoured garlic croûtons.

CUMIN SOUP

The recipe is based on a Tunisian one normally made from dried broad beans. I have replaced the beans with leeks, which make an ideal background to the cumin – the dominating flavour of this soup.

2 tablespoons virgin olive oil
1 teaspoon whole cumin seeds
750 g/1½ lb/3 cups leeks, trimmed, washed & thinly sliced
2 cloves of garlic, peeled & mashed
3 medium potatoes, peeled & coarsely grated
2-3 merguez sausages, dry chorizo or spicy kabanos
2 teaspoons harissa
1 litre/2 pints/4 cups water or stock
salt

1   Heat the oil in a heavy bottomed pan, add the cumin and fry for a minute or two until the seeds start to pop.

2   Add the rest of the ingredients and bring rapidly to the boil. Skim, reduce the heat and simmer for 15-20 minutes. Taste for seasoning. Serve hot.

SPINACH & FETA CHEESE PIE

This simple and quick pie can be served either hot or at room temperature. Take time to clean the fresh spinach thoroughly. Alternatively use chopped frozen spinach.

Filo pastry is available in many supermarkets and can be bought easily either fresh or frozen. Remember the filo dries very quickly and when waiting to be used should be always covered with a slightly dampened cloth.

750 g/1½ lb/3 cups fresh spinach blanched or 500 g/1 lb/2 cups frozen spinach, roughly chopped
250 g/8 oz/1 cup feta cheese, coarsely grated
2 eggs plus 1 egg white, lightly beaten
50 g/2 oz/¼ cup flaked almonds or pine nuts which have been previously browned in a little oil
salt & freshly ground black pepper and a few gratings of nutmeg
10 sheets of filo pastry
4-5 tablespoons olive oil for brushing
1 egg yolk, well beaten together with a pinch of salt & a tablespoon of water
sesame or nigella seeds (optional)

1 Pre-heat the oven to 200°C/400°F/Gas Mark 6.

2 To blanch the spinach, first prepare a large bowl with very cold water. Then fill a large pan with water and 2 teaspoons of salt. Bring to a rapid boil and add half the amount of spinach. Bring back to the boil and then with the help of a slotted spoon or a skimmer remove the spinach directly into the cold water. Repeat with the other half of the spinach. Strain the spinach and gently squeeze it between your hands to exude as much moisture as possible.

3 In a large bowl mix the spinach with the feta cheese, eggs, and egg white, almonds and seasoning.

4 Brush a suitable ovenproof dish with oil and cover the bottom and sides with four sheets of filo pastry, brushing each thoroughly with the oil. Cover them with an even layer of spinach filling. Add another layer of filo, followed by more spinach mixture and finally top with the remaining sheets of filo, brushing each layer with the oil. Trim and tuck in any loose edges, brush with the egg yolk mixture and sprinkle with sesame or nigella seeds.

5 Bake in the oven for 15-20 minutes or until the crust is crisp and golden.

NAVATU EGGS

This recipe is based on one I found in a charming book, *Gibraltar's Favourite Recipes,* published by the Gibraltar League of Hospital Friends. It is wonderfully simple and absolutely delicious. Serve with a simple salad as a first course or light lunch.

6 medium beef tomatoes
3 tablespoons olive oil
2 tablespoons chopped parsley
salt & freshly ground black pepper
100 g / 4 oz / ½ cup raw, dry cured ham such as Prosciutto, jambon de Bayonne
6 large eggs
½ quantity of spicy tomato sauce (see page 11)
rocket leaves to decorate

1 Pre-heat the oven to 180°C/350°F/Gas Mark 4.

2 Remove the top of the tomatoes and set aside. Scoop out the flesh, being careful not to damage the skins.

3 Sprinkle the insides of the tomatoes with half the oil and dust with salt and pepper. Stuff them with half the chopped parsley and with the chopped ham.

4 Place the tomatoes in a well-greased baking tin and carefully break an egg into each. Sprinkle with the rest of the oil and parsley and bake in a medium oven until the eggs are softly set. Serve on a pool of cold spicy tomato sauce, surrounded by a few rocket leaves.

LEEK KUFTADAS

The leek is one of the most ancient of cultivated vegetables. It is mentioned in early Egyptian writing and was one of the ingredients mentioned in the Bible as being missed by the Jews after they left Egypt.

The recipe below is based on a Sephardi Jewish dish, which is traditionally served on the Passover – a holiday associated with the exodus from Egypt.

750 g / 1½ lb / 3 cups leeks, washed & trimmed, with some of the green left on
150 g / 6 oz / ¾ cup feta cheese, coarsely grated or crumbed
3 eggs, beaten
50 g / 2 oz / ¼ cup – 75 g / 3 oz / ⅓ cup matzo meal or bread crumbs
oil for frying

1 Slice the leeks into thin slices and steam them for 3-4 minutes. Rinse under cold water to cool and drain well.

2 Mix the leeks with the feta, eggs and matzo meal. If the mixture is too loose add a bit more matzo meal or bread crumbs. Shape tablespoons of the mixture into flat patties.

3 Heat the oil in a large frying pan and fry the patties for 4-5 minutes on each side or until they are golden brown. Serve warm with Salsa Verde sauce (see page 12).

HERB OMELETTE

Nothing can be simpler, quicker or more refreshing than this omelette. In the eastern Mediterranean appetisingly brilliant green and yellow omelettes are stuffed into pitta bread and sold for you to eat on the streets. When, in the beginning of the summer, fresh green onions are available use those, and use the green leaves too, unless they are shrivelled.

1 large bunch of spring onions or 1 large onion
1 bunch flat-leaf parsley
½ bunch of fresh coriander
6 eggs, beaten with 5 tablespoons water or milk
2 green chillies de-seeded & finely sliced (optional); see below
½ teaspoon ground coriander
½ teaspoon cumin seed
salt & freshly ground pepper
4 tablespoons olive or peanut oil

1 Heat the grill to maximum.

2 Put the onion and washed herbs into a food processor and process, starting and stopping the machine, until chopped but not puréed. Mix in the eggs, sliced chillies, flavouring and salt and pepper.

3 Heat the oil in a heavy bottomed frying pan and pour in the mixture. Allow it to coagulate for a minute and then, like making an omelette, draw the edges into the centre. Reduce the heat to minimum, cover and cook gently for about 5-8 minutes. Uncover and place the frying pan under the heated grill and cook for 5-6 minutes or until the omelette is puffy and has started to brown. Serve very hot or at room temperature.

NOTE When de-seeding chillies it is important to remember that the seeds are the hottest part of the chilli and can cause real damage to sensitive skin, eyes and nose. Either wear gloves or wash your hands thoroughly after dealing with the chillies.

SPRING ONION & TOMATO EGGAH

The term eggah was coined by Claudia Roden and describes a mixture of eggs and various fillings which, when cooked, resemble a crustless quiche. Sliced into small squares, eggah can be served as a light lunch.

The fillings can vary to include cooked vegetables, chicken, meat or liver, pasta, spicy sausage and fish. The following version is my adaptation of a classic recipe. The final grilling of the eggah produces, if served immediately, a wonderful soufflé-like texture.

When making eggah or an omelette do not add the salt to the raw egg mixture as it tends to harden the eggs, making them rubbery; rather sprinkle the cooked dish with salt just before serving.

3 tablespoons good olive oil
2 bunches spring onions, trimmed & roughly chopped
4 medium tomatoes, peeled, de-seeded & roughly chopped
6 eggs, well beaten
100 g / 4 oz / ½ cup Katckaval, Caciocavallo or Pecorino cheese, coarsely grated or cubed
3 tablespoons dill or parsley, chopped
salt & freshly ground black pepper
lemon wedges

1 Pre-heat the grill to maximum.

2 Heat the oil in a heavy bottomed frying pan. Add the spring onions and fry for a minute or two until the onion starts to become transparent. Add the tomatoes, reduce the heat and cook, stirring frequently, for 5 minutes.

3 To the eggs, add the cheese, herbs, and pepper and mix well. Pour the mixture into the frying pan. As the mixture starts to set, draw the set bits into the centre, as you would for an omelette. Go on frying for 5-6 minutes or until the bottom starts to set. Remove from the heat and place under the hot grill. Grill for 5 minutes or until the top is set, fluffy and nicely browned. Either serve immediately or allow to cool to room temperature.

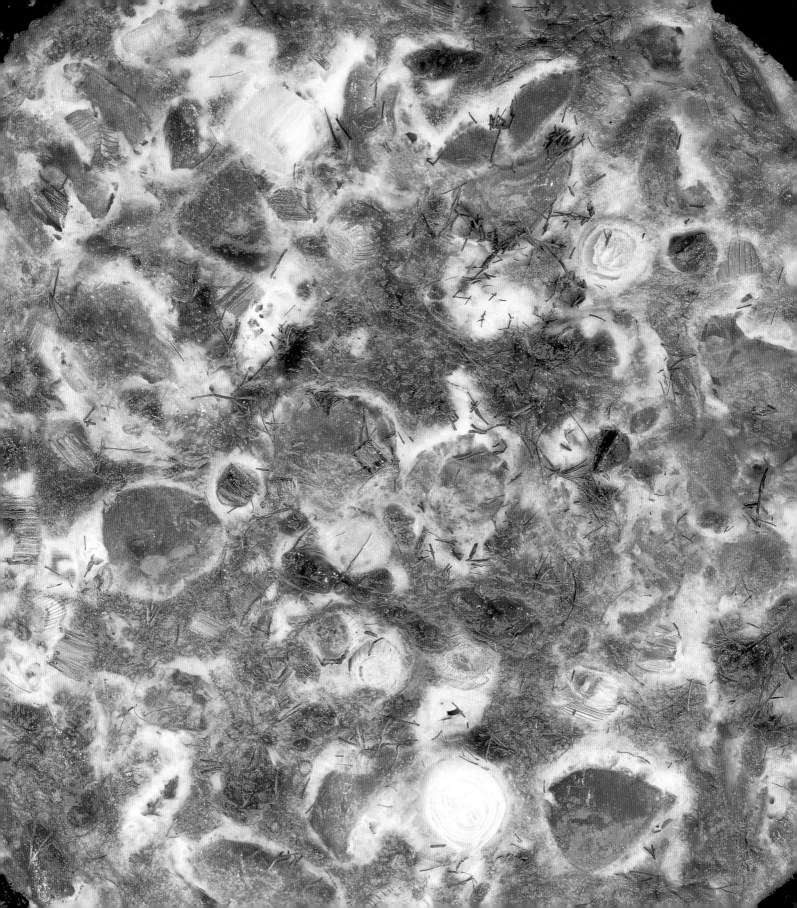

TUNA EGGAH

This recipe does not strictly fit the fresh idea of the book as the tuna used is tinned, but the dish is delicious and tuna is such an essential Mediterranean ingredient. Look around for white meat tuna preserved in either oil or brine which has started to appear on many supermarket shelves. If unobtainable ordinary tinned tuna will do. Unless you are on a diet, use tuna tinned in oil which should be drained thoroughly before use. Serve the eggah on a bed of salad either as a first course or as a main dish in a light lunch or supper.

3 tablespoons olive oil
1 large onion, peeled & coarsely chopped
2 cloves of garlic, peeled & coarsely chopped
2 tins of light meat tuna, well drained & flaked
1 50g/2oz/¼ cup tin of anchovies, drained & chopped
1 tablespoons capers, drained (optional)
6 eggs
3 tablespoons Greek style yogurt
freshly ground black pepper
3 teaspoons chopped dill or parsley
2 medium tomatoes, sliced into rings
lemon wedges for decoration

1   Pre-heat the grill to maximum.

2   Heat the oil in a heavy bottomed frying pan. Add the onion and garlic and fry for a few minutes until the onion starts to change colour. Add the tuna, anchovy and capers and continue frying for a minute or two.

3   Beat the eggs together with the yogurt, seasoning and herbs and pour over the frying mixture. Reduce the heat and, when the edges are starting to set, draw them with the help of a fork toward the centre – like making an omelette. Continue to fry for 2-3 minutes until almost set.

4   Place the sliced tomato on top of the setting mixture. Transfer the pan under the grill for about 5 minutes or until set and nicely browned. Serve decorated with lemon wedges. If more salt is needed sprinkle with a bit of coarse sea salt.

BROAD BEANS SERVED WITH YOGURT

I am always amazed at the variety of fresh legumes available in markets around the Mediterranean. Beans come in a fantastic range of shapes, sizes and colours, and can be used in an equally vast range of salads, first courses, meat stews and soups. This Turkish recipe is a delicious combination of the earthy flavour of broad beans with tart, refreshing and minty yogurt sauce. Shelling broad beans is labour intensive; it is the stuff of family mythology – long summer evenings and children quarrelling over a mountain of beans. Thankfully there is an alternative – buying pre-shelled, frozen ones which, although inferior, do make a reasonable substitute.

1 bunch spring onions, finely chopped
1 tablespoon mint, chopped
juice of 1 lemon
2 tablespoons good virgin olive oil
salt & freshly ground black pepper
750 g / 1½ lb / 3 cups young broad beans, shelled

for the sauce
300 g / 12 oz / 1½ cups Greek style yogurt
juice & grated zest of ½ lemon
2-3 tablespoons good fruity olive oil
1 fat clove of garlic, peeled & mashed
2 tablespoons mint or a combination of mint & parsley, chopped
salt & freshly ground black pepper

for the decoration
1 small purple or white onion, thinly sliced
a few sprigs mint

1   Fill a large pot of water and set over high heat to boil.

2   In a large mixing bowl, combine the spring onion together with the mint, lemon juice, olive oil and seasoning. Mix the dressing well.

3   When the water boils, plunge in the beans, blanch for about 2 minutes and strain. Immediately rinse the beans in cold water. Add the beans to the dressing and mix well.

4   To make the sauce, place the yogurt in a small mixing bowl. Add the other ingredients and mix well. To serve, pile a small mound of beans on individual plates and decorate with the sliced onion and a generous dollop of yogurt. Top with a sprig of mint.

WARM MUSSEL SALAD

Although not traditional the following recipe is purely Mediterranean. It was first thought of as a starter for Christmas dinner but was so successful that it entered my repertoire. It is elegant, light and full of flavour.

100 ml/4 fl.oz/½ cup dry white wine
2 strips orange zest
1 strip grapefruit zest
2 bay leaves
1 teaspoon peppercorns
500 g/1 lb/2 cups mussels, scrubbed & washed
1 large pink grapefruit
2 large oranges
1 small onion, sliced into thin rings

for the dressing
cooking liquid from the mussels
orange & grapefruit juice (see method)
1-2 teaspoon good honey
3 tablespoons hazelnut oil
salt & freshly ground pepper
3 tablespoons chopped dill

1   Place the wine and zests, together with the bay and peppercorns, in a large pan. Bring to the boil, add the mussels and reduce the heat to minimum. Cover and steam for about 5 minutes or until all the mussels are opened and cooked. Lift out the mussels and keep warm. Strain the liquid, and save it for the dressing. Discard any mussels that do not open fully.

2   To segment the grapefruit and oranges, cut a slice from both top and bottom to expose the flesh. Lay the fruit, cut side down, on a chopping board and then, using a serrated knife, slice away the peel exposing the flesh and removing all traces of the white pith. Hold the peeled fruit in the palm of your hand and, with a sharp knife, slice along the vertical membrane lines, leaving a perfectly peeled segment. When all segments are removed, squeeze the juice out of the flesh and reserve. Slice each segment to 2-3 pieces.

3   To make the dressing: place the cooking liquid, fruit juice, honey and oil in a small pan. Bring to the boil, skim, and keep boiling rapidly for 3–4 minutes until glossy and slightly thickened. Season with salt and pepper.

4   In a large salad bowl, mix the mussels with the fruit segments and onions. Pour the boiling sauce over the salad and mix well. Sprinkle the chopped dill and serve with chilled wine and chunky bread.

TARAMASALATA

Please do try to make taramasalata at home. It is easy to make and the results are very different from the pink, over-smooth concoction bought ready made. Originally this delicacy was made from the dried roes of grey mullet. These can be bought for a small fortune at many Greek and Turkish shops and they have a strong gamey flavour which, although deliciously savoury, is very much an acquired taste.

A special tarama paste is also available, which is much cheaper but I find it very salty. Instead I sometimes use smoked cod roe which is readily available at many fishmongers, with very good results. To remove excess saltiness, soak the roes in cold water or milk for a few hours.

Taramasalata is served either as a dip or together with pitta as a light first course. Or, try it, diluted with a bit of yogurt, as an original sauce with grilled fish or plainly boiled vegetables such as leeks, beans or even asparagus.

150 g/6 oz/³⁄4 cup smoked cod roes, all membranes removed
100 g/4 oz/¹⁄2 cup crustless white bread, soaked in water & squeezed dry
1 small onion, finely grated
juice of 1 or more lemons (to taste)
grated zest of ¹⁄2 lemon
150 ml/5 fl.oz/²⁄3 cup extra virgin olive oil or a mixture of olive oil & ground nut oil

1 Put the cod roe, bread, onion, and lemon juice and zest into a food processor and process into a smooth paste.

2 With the machine still running, add the oil in a thin, steady stream and process until a thick cream is achieved. For sauce add either yogurt or cream until a consistency of pouring cream is achieved.

LAMB'S LIVER WITH LEMON & GARLIC

This belongs to a vast range of Turkish and Greek mezé dishes: tender pieces of lamb's liver, pink and juicy, flavoured with lemon, garlic and herbs. Serve it on a toasted pitta or bread so the delicious juices soak in.

Be careful not to overcook the liver because it will become dry and tough. It should be pink in the centre. If lamb's liver is not available use calf's liver.

1 tablespoon sweet paprika
3-4 tablespoons plain flour
500 g / 1 lb / 2 cups lamb's liver, de-veined & cut into
    small pieces
4 tablespoons olive oil
3-4 sprigs of fresh thyme or 1 teaspoon dried thyme

l small onion, peeled & sliced into thin rings
2 cloves of garlic, peeled & finely chopped
juice of 1 large lemon
salt & freshly ground black pepper
1-2 tablespoons chopped flat-leaf parsley
lemon wedges to decorate

1 Mix the paprika together with the flour and dip the liver in the mixture. The easiest way to do it is to put the seasoned flour into a large plastic bag, add the liver and shake well. Discard any loose flour.

2 Heat 3 tablespoons of the oil in a heavy bottomed frying pan. Add the thyme, onion and garlic and fry for a few seconds.

3 Add the seasoned liver and fry for 3–4 minutes, stirring all the time, until the liver is nicely browned. Add the lemon juice and continue frying for about 1 minute.

4 Remove from the heat, sprinkle with the rest of the olive oil, salt, pepper and the parsley. Decorate with lemon wedges and serve either hot or at room temperature.

DEEP FRIED AUBERGINE

These light and crisp fritters are best done just before serving. Other vegetables such as courgettes, courgette flowers, potatoes, carrots, cauliflower, broccoli or young, tender artichokes can be fried in the same way.

Serve with a dip as a snack or on a pool of sauce such as tahina (see page 9) or tarama (see page 40) as a delicious first course.

100 g/4 oz/½ cup plain flour
250 ml/8 fl.oz/1 cup very cold beer or sparkling water
2 tablespoons sesame seeds
1 tablespoon chopped fresh (or 2 teaspoons dry) thyme, savory or tarragon
2 medium aubergines sliced into rounds and then into 1.5 cm/½ in 'chips'
ground nut or sesame oil for deep frying
salt

1 First make the batter. Whisk the flour into the cold beer and add the sesame and herbs and mix well. Allow the mixture to stand in the fridge, covered, for at least 15 minutes.

2 Heat the oil until it is steaming. Drop a few aubergine 'chips' into the cold batter and then into the hot oil and fry for 3-4 minutes until the chips are crisp and golden. Drain well on absorbent paper. Sprinkle with salt and serve hot on a pool of the chosen sauce.

SALADS

PRAWN & ORANGE SALAD

The inspiration for this unusual combination comes from Morocco. There, the salad is made from a local variety of aromatic oranges which have a delightful, slightly bitter flavour. They are simply peeled, sliced and mixed with onion and a dressing of olive oil.

The salad below can be made with any good sharp oranges and makes a refreshing dish to serve either as a light lunch or as an elegant first course.

3 tablespoons virgin olive or walnut oil
juice of 1 small orange
1 teaspoon grated orange zest
salt & freshly ground black pepper
3 large oranges, peeled & sliced into thin rings
1 bunch of spring onions, trimmed & chopped
300 g / 12 oz / 1½ cups cooked peeled prawns
3 tablespoons dill

1   In a large salad bowl combine the oil with the orange juice, zest and the seasoning and mix well.

2   Add the rest of the ingredients and toss gently. Serve decorated with a few unpeeled prawns and sprigs of dill.

SALATA DE PIPINO (CUCUMBER SALAD)

This pale green and refreshing salad is ideal for serving with fish dishes. The best cucumbers to use are the small, sweet, hard, intensely green variety imported from the Mediterranean.

Traditionally this salad is flavoured with white pepper but, if you are like me and do not mind little black specks in your salad, use black pepper as it is more aromatic.

3 tablespoons white wine vinegar
2 tablespoons water
1 clove of garlic, mashed
salt & freshly ground black pepper
1-2 teaspoons sugar or honey (optional)
500 g / 1 lb / 2 cups cucumber
2 tablespoons chopped dill or mint

1   Mix the dressing in a large salad bowl.

2   Slice the cucumber into paper thin rounds, add to the dressing together with the chopped herbs, mix well and serve.

RAW ARTICHOKE SALAD

This attractive salad has a surprisingly fresh, earthy flavour and goes very well with cold or cured meats, poached egg or just bread and butter for a light and elegant supper dish. It comes from the North African coast of the Mediterranean, where artichokes are supposed to have healing powers. The water in which the artichokes are cooked is drunk to improve health and help with problems of potency and fertility.

To clean the artichokes, first peel all the leaves exposing the chokey heart. With a sharp teaspoon scrape away the choke. Trim, and remove the stem if too woody. Immediately plunge the peeled artichoke into cold acidulated water as the cut surface blackens very quickly. Do not throw away the leaves; use them to decorate the salad.

4 large artichokes, cleaned as above
1 bunch spring onions
2 large tomatoes, peeled, de-seeded & roughly chopped
3 tablespoons virgin olive oil
juice of 1 lemon or to taste
1 clove of garlic, finely chopped
½ lemon sliced into thin slices, each slice cut into small wedges
salt & freshly ground black pepper
3 tablespoons parsley, roughly chopped

1 Peel the artichokes as explained above.

2 Combine the rest of the ingredients in a large salad bowl and mix well. Slice the artichokes into thin crescents and immediately coat with the dressing. Decorate with artichoke leaves and serve. The salad improves if left to marinate for a few hours. The artichoke hearts will not discolour once they are coated in the dressing.

COOKED BEANS & TOMATO SALAD

Cooked vegetable salads are eaten all around the Mediterranean. They can be served hot but are at their best at room temperature.

4 tablespoons strong olive oil
250 g/8 oz/1 cup onion, coarsely chopped
5-8 fat cloves of garlic, peeled & coarsely chopped
1-2 green or red chillies, sliced (optional)
4 medium tomatoes, peeled, de-seeded & coarsely chopped
salt
500 g/1 lb/2 cups fine French beans, topped & tailed
chopped parsley & lemon wedges for decoration

1 Heat the oil in a heavy bottomed frying pan. Add the onion, garlic and chillies and fry over high heat for about 4-5 minutes or until the garlic starts to brown.

2 Add the tomatoes and salt. Reduce the heat and simmer, stirring, for a few minutes.

3 Add the beans, mix well, cover the pan and steam for 8-10 minutes, stirring the mixture once or twice. The beans should remain crunchy. Serve in a warmed dish, decorated with lemon wedges and parsley.

CELERY & TOMATO SALAD

This salad is colourful, easy to make and delicious as an accompaniment to a main course.

The best celery to use is the green leafy variety that is easily obtained from Greek and Indian grocers.

3 tablespoons olive oil
juice of 1 lemon
salt
1 large head of celery, trimmed and chopped
2 large beef tomatoes
100 g/4 oz/1/2 cup black olives, chopped
2 tablespoons chopped flat-leaf parsley

1 In a large salad bowl mix the oil, lemon juice and salt.

2 Add the rest of the ingredients and mix well.

AUBERGINE & TOMATO SALAD

The aubergine is one of the essential ingredients of the Mediterranean kitchen. It is made into numerous salads, dips and pastes, stuffed, stewed and even made into a delicious sweet jam and into preserves.

The following recipe is a particularly healthy and unusual combination of cooked aubergine and fresh tomatoes.

4 tablespoons good olive oil
1 large onion, peeled & finely chopped
3 cloves of garlic, peeled & chopped
1 or more red chillies, de-seeded & sliced
a few strips of lemon zest
750 g/1½ lb/3 cups aubergine, trimmed and cubed
300 g/12 oz/1½ cups tomatoes, grated on a coarse grater
salt & freshly ground black pepper
3 tablespoons parsley or mint, chopped
2 tablespoons olive oil
lemon wedges

1   Heat the first quantity of oil in a heavy bottomed frying pan, add the onion, garlic, chillies and lemon zest and fry, on high heat, for 3-4 minutes, stirring constantly.

2   In the meantime, put the cubed aubergine into the food processor and process, starting and stopping the machine until the mixture is finely chopped but not puréed. Add the aubergine to the pan, reduce the heat, cover and simmer for about 15 minutes.

3   Uncover and season. Increase the heat and cook for a few more minutes until most of the liquid has evaporated. Switch the heat off and remove the lemon zest. Add the tomatoes and herbs and mix well. Turn into a serving dish, sprinkle with the olive oil, decorate with lemon wedges and serve.

NOTE: When dealing with chillies it is important to remember that the seeds (the hottest part) can cause real damage to sensitive skin, to the eyes and nose. Either wear gloves to chop chillies or make sure you wash your hands thoroughly after handling them.

MOROCCAN LEMON SALAD

If, like me, you love lemon this is the salad for you. It is delightfully tart and goes very well with any fried or grilled fish especially with the oilier ones like sardines and mackerels. The relish improves with storing. It will keep in the fridge for up to two weeks.

You can peel the lemons if you don't like things too bitter, in which case include some grated zest to intensify the lemony flavour.

4 ripe, thin-skinned lemons
2 teaspoons olive oil
2 teaspoons or more harissa (see page 9)
1 bunch flat-leaf parsley, chopped

1   Slice the lemons into thin rounds, discarding any pips.

2   Add the rest of the ingredients and mix well.

PANZANELLA

As a child I ate my salad only because at the end I could dunk bread into the wonderfully savoury juice that the vegetables produce. When I grew up I discovered Panzanella – a way of enjoying the tasty combination of olive oil, lemon and tomato juices – without dunking the bread.

This is a clever way of using stale bread and making a salad into a more substantial dish, ideal as a light summer lunch with a glass of chilled white wine.

Bread salads are eaten all around the Mediterranean and they differ in the types of bread used. Panzanella is made from stale Tuscan bread in Italy; in Greece and Turkey, pitta is used. I like to make the salad from the soft, round pitta that has started to appear in many shops and supermarkets. Whatever bread you choose, make sure that it is a good quality, traditionally-baked loaf.

5 tablespoons good olive oil
juice of 1 large lemon, or more to taste
3 tablespoons water
salt & freshly ground black pepper
4 medium, ripe tomatoes, peeled & sliced
1 large purple onion, sliced
1 large red pepper, cored & sliced
4 round pittas or 6 slices of tasty, good white bread
1 large bunch of flat-leaf parsley, leaves only, chopped or
*   ½ bunch of parsley & the same quantity basil*

1   In a large salad bowl combine the oil, lemon juice, water and seasoning. Add the vegetables and toss well.

2   Tear the pitta or bread into small pieces and add to the salad, together with the chopped herbs and mix well. Allow the salad to stand for about 10 minutes for the bread to soak up the juices. Taste the salad and add more lemon and salt if necessary as bread tends to neutralise acidity.

FRIED SPINACH SALAD

Spinach is one of the most popular vegetables around the Mediterranean. It appears in salads and stuffings, adds colour to pasta or gnocchi and is served to accompany meat or fish.

The word spinach is sometimes misleading as it is used as a collective term to describe green edible leaves. I like making the dish from chard or beet leaves which have an intense, earthy flavour and are less muddy therefore need less preparation. Chard and beet are available almost all year round in many Indian, Greek and Turkish grocers.

1 kg/2 lb/4 cups chard or spinach, washed well
2 medium onions, peeled & chopped
4 tablespoons good olive oil
salt & freshly ground pepper
a few scrapings of nutmeg
juice of 1 orange
grated zest of 1/2 orange
1 tablespoon olive oil
50 g/2 oz/1/4 cup pine nuts previously browned in a bit of oil
lemon wedges

1   Wash the spinach in a few changes of water, remove tough stems and wilted leaves and chop coarsely. If using chard – wash and trim the stems, lay a few leaves on top of each other, roll into a thick cigar shape and slice across thinly.

2   In a heavy bottomed frying pan heat half the first quantity of oil. Add half the onion and fry for a minute or two until the onion starts to become transparent. Add half of the spinach and fry, on high flame, for about 4-5 minutes until the leaves wilt and most of the liquid has evaporated. Lift into a serving dish. Repeat with the rest of the spinach, the onion and the oil.

3   Add the seasoning, dress with orange juice, orange zest and olive oil and mix well. Decorate with the pine nuts and lemon wedges and serve either warm or at room temperature.

AHIVETCH OR GAIVETCH

This delicious cooked vegetable salad is probably of Turkish origin but appears, in many guises, all over the Mediterranean. Any seasonal vegetables are healthy and ideally suited to this piquant concoction. When grapes are plentiful I like to add some seedless green ones as they add a delightful sweetness.

3 tablespoons olive oil
1 large onion, peeled & chopped
3 cloves of garlic, peeled & chopped
3-4 celery stems, coarsely chopped
150 g/6 oz/³⁄4 cup French beans, topped, tailed & sliced
2 courgettes, sliced into rings
1 red & 1 green pepper, de-seeded & sliced into strips
100 g/4 oz/¹⁄2 cup fresh peas
75 g/3 oz/¹⁄3 cup seedless grapes (optional)
2 large tomatoes, peeled, de-seeded & coarsely chopped
a few sprigs of fresh oregano, savory & tarragon or ¹⁄2 teaspoon each of dried chopped parsley

1   Heat the oil in a heavy bottomed frying pan. Add the onion and garlic and
    fry for a few minutes or until the onion starts to take colour.

2   Add the vegetables (and grapes), stir well and
    reduce the heat. Continue frying for about
    10-15 minutes. Add the tomato and herbs,
    increase the heat and continue frying for a
    minute or two until the tomato is hot.
    Serve decorated with chopped
    parsley either warm or at
    room temperature.

LAMB STEAKS WITH FRESH APRICOT SAUCE

The combination of young tender lamb and apricots is magical. It appears in many forms around the Mediterranean. In North Africa it is made into a delicious tagine (stew) and in Jerusalem I once had apricots stuffed with minced lamb and cooked in a sweet and sour sauce.

The following dish is a modern interpretation of this age old combination. When fresh apricots are not in season, dried apricots which have previously soaked in hot water can be used.

2 tablespoons honey
2 tablespoons olive oil
4-6 lamb steaks, each weighing about 150 g/6 oz
salt & freshly ground black pepper

for the sauce
500 g/1 lb/2 cups fresh apricots, kernels removed or
150 g/6 oz/³/4 cup dried apricots
1-2 tablespoons honey (to taste)
2 tablespoons chopped fresh mint (or 1 tablespoon dried)
a few drops of lemon juice
¹/2 teaspoon grated lemon zest
salt & freshly ground black pepper

a few sprigs of fresh mint for decoration

1   Heat the grill to maximum. Mix the honey with the oil and brush over the steaks. Season with salt and pepper. Grill at a high heat for 4-5 minutes each side. This will result in medium rare lamb steaks; if you like your lamb well done, grill for a few minutes more.

2   Put all the sauce ingredients into a food processor and process into a smooth purée.

3   Decorate each steak with a sprig of mint and serve on a pool of sauce.

BARBECUED SHISH KEBABS

In my memory Mediterranean evenings are always associated with the sweet smell of jasmine and the irresistible, appetising aroma of barbecuing meats. Sweet herbs and aromatic woods are used to impart special flavour to anything cooked on them.

A barbecue is a full meal which can include barbecued vegetables, mushrooms and cheese to start with, followed by fish, seafood, meat and sausages and all served with fresh salads, bread, and, depending where you come from, large quantities of wine, ouzo, raki or beer.

Modern gas barbecues are convenient and easier to use, but if you have the time, do it the traditional way with good hardwood coals. And do experiment with different aromatic herbs such as rosemary branches, thyme or even lavender. These should be placed on the hot coals just before adding the meats.

This recipe is of Lebanese origin. Serve with Tahina sauce (see page 9), a pilav of burgul or rice for a main course or lunch.

1 medium onion, peeled & quartered
1 small clove of garlic, mashed
½ bunch flat-leaf parsley, stems removed
1-2 green chillies, trimmed & de-seeded (optional)
750 g / 1½ lb / 3 cups ground lean lamb or beef
2-3 tablespoons good olive oil
a pinch of cinnamon
¼ teaspoon allspice
¼ teaspoon ground cardamom (optional)
salt & freshly ground pepper

1   Place the onion, garlic and chilli (if used) in a food processor and process, starting and stopping the machine, until finely chopped but not puréed

2   Transfer into a mixing bowl, add the rest of the ingredients and mix very well.

3   With wet hands shape into thick kebabs. Either grill or barbecue for about 7-8 minutes each side for a rare kofta, 10 for a medium or longer still if liked. Serve immediately with a pilav, fresh salad and Tahina sauce.

COFTAS COOKED IN TAHINA SAUCE

A delicious dish of Lebanese origin which can be served either as a main course or as a appetising starter.

1 medium onion, peeled
2 cloves of garlic, peeled
½ bunch flat-leaf parsley, leaves only
500 g / 1 lb / 2 cups raw minced lamb
50 g / 2 oz / ¼ cup bread crumbs
1 egg
½ teaspoon allspice
salt & freshly ground black pepper
1 quantity of tahina sauce (see page 9), diluted with 50 g / 2 oz / ¼ cup of water
1 tablespoon each of pine nuts & parsley for decoration

1   Heat the grill to maximum and heat the oven to 220°C/425°F/Gas Mark 7.

2   Put the onion, garlic and parsley into the food processor and process, turning the machine on and off, until roughly chopped. Transfer into a large mixing bowl and add the rest of the ingredients except the tahina and decoration. Mix well.

3   Wet your hands and shape the mixture into 5 cm/2 in coftas, like round sausages. Grill the coftas for 4-5 minutes each side. They should just remain pink inside.

4   Arrange the coftas in a greased, oven proof dish. Pour the tahina over and bake for about 10 minutes or until the tahina is bubbling and starts to brown. Decorate with pine nuts which have previously browned in a little oil and parsley. Serve hot with rice or burgul.

LAMB COFTAS COOKED WITH LEMON & CUMIN

Around the Mediterranean meat used to be an expensive commodity. Large joints were cooked only for special celebrations or on Sunday. For everyday food many techniques of 'stretching' meat were developed. Minced meat was bulked with either bread or rice and burgul. The addition of chopped herbs and vegetables to the mixture produces light, healthier coftas, being reduced in saturated fat content. The following recipe comes from Morocco.

1 large onion, sliced
1 large bunched of flat-leaf parsley, tough stems removed
2-3 sticks of green celery (see below)
500 g / 1 lb / 2 cups very lean lamb, minced
1 egg
2 tablespoons virgin olive oil
75 g / 3 oz / 1/3 cup fresh bread crumbs or soaked burgul
1/4 teaspoon whole cumin seeds
olive oil for frying

for the sauce
3 tablespoons olive oil
1/4 teaspoon whole cumin seeds
1 medium onion, finely chopped
1 clove of garlic, finely chopped
250 ml / 8 fl.oz / 1 cup stock or dry white wine
2 teaspoons tomato purée
1 small lemon, peeled & sliced into small cubes
salt & freshly ground black pepper

1 tablespoon chopped parsley for decoration

1   Heat the grill to maximum.

2   Put the onion, parsley and celery into a food processor and process, switching the machine on and off, until the mixture is chopped but not puréed. Transfer the mixture into a mixing bowl and add the rest of the main ingredients. Mix thoroughly.

3   Shape into 12 thickish patties and grill for about 5 minutes on each side. The coftas should remain slightly pink inside.

4   Meanwhile, to prepare the sauce: heat the oil in a heavy bottomed frying pan. Add the cumin and fry over high heat for a second or two. Add the onion and the garlic and continue frying until the onion starts to change colour. Add the remaining ingredients, bring to the boil and boil for 5 minutes.

5   When the coftas are ready pour the boiling sauce over them. Decorate with chopped parsley and serve immediately accompanied by rice burgul or a salad.

NOTE   Dark green leaf celery is available in many Greek, Turkish and Indian shops. It has a strong celery flavour and is used for cooking rather than eating raw. If unavailable the 'American' variety will do.

VEAL IN ANCHOVY & CAPER SAUCE

Veal is much loved by the Italians, but I find the butter and cream which are associated with veal cooking much too heavy. The following is an adaptation of an Italian classic with neither. Served on a bed of pasta it makes a light, healthy and delicious main course.

500 g / 1 lb / 2 cups veal escalopes, thinly sliced but not pounded
flour for dusting
4 tablespoons good olive oil
1 large onion, peeled & coarsely chopped
3 cloves garlic, peeled & coarsely chopped
2 tablespoons capers, rinsed & coarsely chopped
1x50 g / 2 oz tin of anchovies, drained & roughly chopped
1-2 strips of lemon zest
500 g / 1 lb / 2 cups plum tomatoes, skinned, de-seeded & roughly chopped
150 ml / 6 fl.oz / ³/4 cup white wine
salt & freshly ground pepper
500 g / 1 lb / 2 cups tagliatelle or spaghetti
3 tablespoons chopped flat-leaf parsley

1   Slice the escalopes into thick strips about 2.5 cm/1 in wide. Dust with flour.

2   Heat 3 tablespoons of the oil in a heavy bottomed frying pan. Add the veal slices, a few at a time, and fry over a medium heat for about 2-3 minutes on each side or until nicely browned. Do not over-crowd the pan. Lift them into a warmed dish and keep warm.

3   Add the rest of the oil, together with onion, garlic, capers, anchovies and lemon zest. Fry for a few minutes, mixing frequently. Add the tomatoes and the wine, season and bring to the boil. Reduce the heat and simmer for about 10-15 minutes.

4   Cook the pasta according to the manufacturer's instructions. When ready drain well and keep hot. Add the escalopes to the simmering sauce, heat through, season and arrange on a bed of pasta. Sprinkle with parsley and serve.

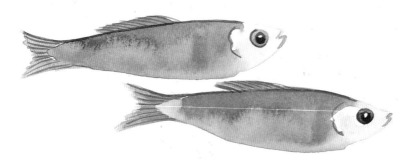

CHICKEN COOKED WITH OLIVES & ORANGE

The combination of tart orange with the salty bitterness of the olives and the chicken is magic. Serve it hot with either rice, burgul or couscous.

100 g / 4 oz / ½ cup broken green olives (see below)
4-6 boneless chicken breasts, skin removed
100 g / 4 oz / ½ cup flour seasoned with salt,
   freshly ground black pepper and 1 teaspoon paprika
4 tablespoons olive oil
1 large onion, peeled & finely chopped
100 ml / 4 fl. oz / ½ cup dry white wine
250 ml / 8 fl. oz / 1 cup chicken stock or water
juice of 3 tart oranges
grated zest of 1 orange
1 teaspoon freshly ground coriander
salt & freshly ground black pepper
2 tablespoons coriander leaves for decoration

1   Soak the olives in boiling water for 20 minutes.

2   With a sharp knife make 3 gashes in each chicken breast and dip them in the seasoned flour. Set aside.

3   Heat the oil in a shallow, heavy bottomed pan. Add the onion and chicken breast and fry for a few minutes until onion starts to turn colour. Add the wine, chicken stock, juice, zest and ground coriander. Bring to the boil, reduce the heat and simmer gently for 20 minutes.

4   Add the olives and the seasoning, increase the heat and boil rapidly for about 5 minutes until the sauce is reduced and shiny. Serve with rice, couscous or burgul decorated with chopped coriander leaves.

NOTE   Available in many Italian, Greek and Mediterranean grocers.

CHICKEN BREAST COOKED WITH PEPPERS & SUN DRIED TOMATOES

This flavoursome dish is delicious either hot or served cold as a delightful summer lunch dish. Rice or burgul pilaf goes well with the rich Mediterranean tang of the peppers.

4 tablespoons good olive oil
1 large onion, peeled & thinly sliced
4 cloves of garlic, peeled & roughly sliced
2 red peppers, de-seeded & sliced into a fine julienne
2 green peppers, de-seeded & sliced into a fine julienne
75 g/3 oz/1/3 cup sun dried tomatoes in oil, sliced into thin julienne
300 ml/12 fl. oz/1 1/2 cups boiling chicken stock or water
500 g/1 lb chicken breast, sliced into 1 cm/1/2 in strips
salt & freshly ground black pepper
2 tablespoons chopped coriander leaves

1   Heat the oil in a heavy bottomed frying pan and add the onion, garlic and the peppers. Fry over a medium heat for a few minutes or until the onion starts to change colour. Add the tomatoes and their oil, together with the stock, bring to the boil, reduce the heat and simmer, covered, for 10 minutes.

2   Season the chicken with salt and pepper. Increase the heat of the pepper and tomato mixture, add the chicken and go on cooking, stirring all the time, for about 5 minutes or until the chicken is done and most of the liquid has evaporated. Check the seasoning and sprinkle with coriander and serve.

CHICKEN LIVER PILAV

The first time I ate this pilav was at a beautifully situated house overlooking the Bosphorus. It's a delicious and subtle concoction of crunchy nuts and melting chicken liver. With a green-leaf salad it makes a delightful summer main course.

5 tablespoons olive oil or butter
350 g / 14 oz / 1¾ cups long grain rice
1 litre / 2 pints / 4 cups boiling chicken stock or water
50 g / 2 oz / ¼ cup sultanas
50 g / 2 oz / ¼ cup almonds
50 g / 2 oz / ¼ cup pine nuts
300 g / 12 oz chicken liver, sliced into
  2.5 cm / 1 in pieces
1 large onion, peeled & thinly sliced
salt & freshly ground black pepper
2 tablespoons chopped dill

1   Heat 2 tablespoons of the oil in a heavy bottomed pan, add the rice and fry over high heat for a minute or two or until the rice starts changing colour and becomes opaquely white. Add the boiling stock and sultanas and bring to the boil. Reduce the heat, cover and simmer for 15-20 minutes or until the liquid has been absorbed and the rice is tender.

2   Heat the rest of the oil in a heavy bottomed frying pan, add the almonds and pine nuts and fry for a minute or two until the nuts are nicely brown. Lift out and reserve. Add the livers and onion and fry for about 5 minutes until the liver is just cooked; the inside should remain pink and juicy. Season with salt and pepper.

3   Fold the nuts, liver mixture and dill into the rice, mix and fluff up with a fork, and serve immediately.

BURGUL PILAV

Burgul, mistakenly known as cracked wheat, is probably the most ancient convenience food. It is made from pre-cooked and dried wheat and, although this recipe *is* cooked, needs no cooking. Burgul is used a lot in the eastern part of the Mediterranean.

3 tablespoons olive oil
1 small onion, chopped
300 g / 12 oz / 1½ cups coarse grained burgul
750 ml / 1½ pints / 3 cups boiling water
Salt to taste

1 Heat the oil in a shallow pan. Add the onion and fry gently until soft and golden.

2 Add the burgul and continue frying, stirring frequently, for 2-3 minutes or until it begins to change colour. Add the boiling water and salt and stir well. Bring to the boil, reduce the heat and cover tightly. Simmer very gently for 15-20 minutes or until all the water is absorbed. Leave to rest, covered, for 10 minutes and serve.

MUSHROOM & PANCETTA PASTA

Mushroom madness spreads through Italy in spring and again in autumn. Woods are alive with the mushroom gatherers, and wild mushrooms have an extraordinary flavour and aroma, the mixture of which gets the taste buds going.

The first time I tasted this dish, it was made from porcini; even they are expensive in Italy. A combination of brown cup and dried porcini works very well, and the dried funghi are now available in most supermarkets or in Italian grocers.

2 tablespoons olive oil
1 large onion, peeled & coarsely chopped
250 g/8 oz/1 cup pancetta, coarsely diced
15 g/1/2 oz dried porcini, soaked in boiling water
*   for 30 minutes*
500 g/1 lb/2 cups brown cup or large field
*   mushrooms, wiped clean & thinly sliced*
1 tablespoon dark soy sauce
400 ml/14 fl.oz/1 1/2 cups chicken stock or water
salt & freshly ground black pepper
750 g/1 1/2 lb/3 cups fresh or dried tagliatelle or
*   farfalle*

to finish
grated zest of 1/2 lemon
2 tablespoons flat-leaf parsley, finely chopped
2 cloves of garlic, peeled & finely chopped
grated Parmesan cheese

1   Heat the oil in a heavy bottomed frying pan and add the onion. Fry until it starts to change colour. Add the pancetta and fry for a few more minutes.

2   Drain the porcini, and chop them finely. Add them to the pan with the sliced fresh mushrooms. Fry for 5 minutes longer, mixing well until the mushrooms have just softened.

3   Add the soy sauce and the stock, season and bring to the boil. Reduce the heat and simmer for about 15-20 minutes or until most of the liquid has evaporated.

4   Meanwhile, boil the pasta according to the manufacturer's instructions. Drain well and add to the pan, together with the lemon zest, parsley and garlic. Mix gently with a fork, heat through and serve immediately. Put a generous bowl of Parmesan cheese on the table.

PASTA WITH SPICY ITALIAN SAUSAGES

Sausages are a most convenient fast food. Around the Mediterranean, where sausages were probably invented, they are used as instant flavouring for numerous stews and dishes. Smoked, spicy or mild sausages are added either fresh or dried to spike and flavour bland ingredients such as grain, beans, vegetables or pasta. The following recipe comes from Italy and calls for spicy-hot cooking sausage which is normally sold, in Italian delicatessens, under the name of 'Piquante' or peperone. If unobtainable any spicy *chorizo* type sausage will do.

3 tablespoons good olive oil
2 large onions, peeled & roughly chopped
4 fat cloves garlic, peeled & roughly chopped
3 strips lemon or orange zest
500 g/1 lb/2 cups spicy sausage, cut into large chunks
500 g/1 lb/2 cups plum tomatoes, peeled, de-seeded & roughly chopped
250 ml/8 fl.oz/1 cup robust red wine
salt & freshly ground pepper
750 g/1½ lb/3 cups pappardelle or wide fettucine
½ bunch of flat-leaf parsley, roughly chopped

1   Heat the oil in a large, heavy-bottomed frying pan. Add the onion and garlic and fry for a few minutes until the onion starts to change colour. Add the lemon zest and sausage and fry for a few minutes more. Add the tomatoes and the wine, bring to the boil, reduce the heat and simmer over medium heat for about 20 minutes or until the sausages are cooked and the liquid much reduced.

2   Cook the pasta according to the manufacturer's directions. Pour the sauce over the pasta, sprinkle with plenty of parsley and serve immediately.

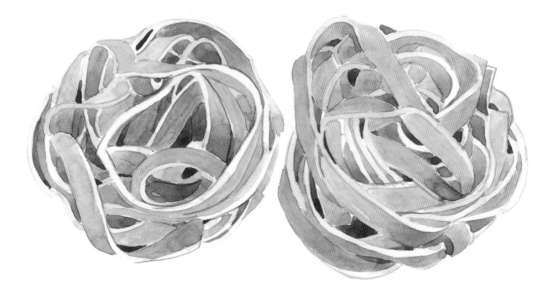

BREAST OF BARBARY DUCK IN TAMARIND SAUCE

Barbary ducks are said to have originated in the Barbary Mountains of North Africa; in fact they were developed in the South of France and are now available at the speciality meat counters of most big supermarkets.

Tamarind or Indian date is the sour pulp which surrounds the seeds of the tamarind tree. It is sold in most Indian and oriental stores, either as a compressed slab or as a paste. The paste is the easiest to use as, in the other form, the tamarind needs to be soaked in hot water and sieved to get rid of the seeds. Tamarind was introduced to the eastern Mediterranean from India and it was popularly used as a souring agent and as the base of many sauces, refreshing drinks and sorbets. Its fruity tang makes it ideal for the gamey flavour of the Barbary duck.

This is my adaptation of an ancient Italian recipe.

4-6 boneless breasts of Barbary duck
1 tablespoon fragrant honey
3 tablespoons good olive oil
100 g/4 oz/½ cup shallots, peeled & quartered
2 cloves of garlic, peeled & roughly sliced
2 tablespoons tamarind paste
2 teaspoons honey or brown sugar
150 ml/6 fl.oz/¾ cup chicken stock
50 g/2 oz/¼ cup fruity red wine
50 g/2 oz/¼ cup currants
salt & freshly ground black pepper

1 Heat the grill to maximum.

2 Make 3 deep slashes in each breast and brush with the honey. Grill the duck breasts for 4 minutes on each side, place on a warmed dish, and keep hot.

3 Heat the oil in a heavy bottomed frying pan. Add the shallots and garlic and fry until the shallots start to change colour. Mix the tamarind together with the honey, stock and wine and add to the pan. Add the currants, season and bring to the boil. Reduce the heat and simmer for 15 minutes.

4 Increase the heat, and boil rapidly for about 3-4 minutes until the sauce is thickened and shiny. Add the duck and continue cooking for a minute or two, frequently turning in the sauce. If you like your duck well done continue cooking until done to your liking, for about a further 5 minutes.

TUNA SERVED WITH PEPPER & OLIVE SAUCE

Since antiquity the dark, veal-like flesh of the tuna has been admired all over the Mediterranean. This French recipe is typical of the Côte d'Azur.

Fresh tuna should be treated carefully; when cooked for too long the flesh becomes dry and unpleasant. Therefore cook it until pink, rather than grey, just like lamb or beef.

If fresh tuna is not available, sword fish, which is plentiful in the sea all over the region, can be used instead.

4-6 tuna steaks each weighing about 150 g / 6 oz
50 g / 2 oz / ¼ cup seasoned flour for dredging
4 tablespoons good olive oil
1 clove of garlic, peeled & crushed
1 red pepper, sliced into a thin julienne
3 anchovy fillets, chopped
100 g / 4 oz / ½ cup black olives, pitted & chopped
100 ml / 4 fl.oz / ½ cup stock
salt & freshly ground black pepper
juice of ½ a lemon
3 tablespoons dill or flat-leaf parsley, chopped

1 Dip the tuna steaks in the seasoned flour.

2 Heat half the oil in a heavy bottomed frying pan, add the tuna and fry over high heat for 2 minutes. Turn the steaks over and fry for a further 2 minutes. Remove and keep warm.

3 Add the rest of the oil and the garlic and red pepper and fry for a minute or two until the garlic starts to change colour. Add the anchovies, olives and the stock, and bring to the boil. Reduce the heat and simmer for about 10 minutes.

4 Increase the heat, add the tuna steaks and cook over a high heat for 4–5 minutes. Baste the steaks frequently with the cooking liquid. If you like your tuna well done continue to cook until the flesh is just flaking. Immediately before serving, season and sprinkle with the lemon juice and the chopped herbs.

FISH COOKED IN A SPICY TOMATO SAUCE

This tasty and easy recipe comes from Tunis. The fish is first lightly fried and then cooked in spicy tomato sauce. Other fish suitable for this treatment include cod, salmon or tuna, but it is especially good with grey mullet. Serve the fish with rice, couscous or burgul and a chilled glass or two of dry white wine.

Olive oil for shallow frying
75 g/3 oz/¹/₃ cup flour
2 teaspoons sweet paprika
scant teaspoon salt
¹/₂ teaspoon freshly ground black pepper
4-6 fish steaks
¹/₂ bunch of flat-leaf parsley
¹/₂ quantity spicy tomato sauce (see page 11)
juice & grated zest of 1 lemon
lemon wedges & chopped parsley for decoration

1 Heat the oil in a heavy bottomed frying pan. Mix the flour with the seasoning and dust the fish well. Fry the steaks in the hot oil for a few minutes each side until the pieces are nicely golden. Lift out and drain on absorbent paper.

2 Arrange the chopped parsley at the bottom of a large, heavy bottomed pan and arrange the fish on top. Add the tomato sauce, juice and grated zest of the lemon, mix well and pour over the fish. Bring to the boil, reduce the heat and simmer very gently for 15 minutes. Decorate with lemon wedges and parsley and serve either hot or at room temperature.

GRILLED FISH SERVED WITH TARAMASALATA

This recipe was invented in a moment of desperation. Once on holiday, a friend arrived with a fresh catch and the fridge, except for a covered jar of home made tarama, was empty like an Arctic desert. Since then the dish has developed into a remarkably subtle combination of flavours and textures.

4-6 medium white-fleshed fish, each weighing about
150 g/6 oz–250 g/8 oz, cleaned & washed well
3 tablespoons lemon juice
salt
olive oil for brushing

for the tarama (see page 40 & use half the quantity
50 g/2 oz/¹/₄ cup–75 g/3 oz/¹/₃ cup yogurt, cream
or milk
parsley and lemon wedges for decoration

1 Heat the grill to maximum.

2 Make 3 deep slashes on each side of the fish and sprinkle, both outside and inside, with lemon juice and salt. Arrange the fish in the grill pan, brush with oil and grill for 8-10 minutes. Turn the fish, brush with oil and grill for a further 8-10 minutes or until the fish is ready.

3 For the sauce, dilute the tarama with the yogurt, cream or milk.

4 Pour a small ladle of the sauce on each plate. Place the fish on it and serve garnished with parsley leaves and lemon wedges.

PRAWNS IN TOMATO & CHILLI SAUCE

This recipe was inspired by a classic Provençal dish. Use good quality raw prawns. You can peel them before cooking but the result will be a bit insipid.

3 tablespoons olive oil
½ teaspoon whole fennel seeds
100 g/4 oz/½ cup shallots, peeled & chopped
3 cloves of garlic, peeled & roughly chopped
1-2 red or green chillies
2 bay leaves
2 strips of lemon zest

2 large, ripe beef tomatoes, peeled, de-seeded &
    roughly chopped
150 ml/6 fl.oz/¾ cup fish stock or dry white wine
500 g/1 lb/2 cups raw prawns
salt & freshly ground black pepper
2 tablespoons chopped dill

1   Heat the oil in a heavy bottomed frying pan. Add the fennel seeds and fry for a minute or two or until the seeds start to pop. Add the shallots, garlic, chillies, bay leaves and lemon zest and fry over high heat for a minute or two. Add the tomatoes and stock, bring to the boil, reduce the heat and simmer for 5 minutes.

2   Increase the heat and add the prawns. Season and continue cooking, stirring frequently, for about 5-8 minutes or until the prawns are just done. Serve hot on a bed of rice, couscous or burgul, and sprinkle over the chopped dill.

BAKED SEA BASS

Sea bass is one of the most treasured fish of the Mediterranean. It has a delicate moist flesh which maintains its shape after cooking. This is one of the best and easiest ways of cooking sea bass.

I have used grated fresh ginger which is not traditional in the Mediterranean kitchen, although in its dry form it is used extensively, appearing in savoury as well as sweet recipes.

1 large sea bass, weighing about 1½ kg/3 lb
3 tablespoons parsley, roughly chopped
1 tablespoon thyme, chopped
2 cloves of garlic, peeled & finely chopped
juice & grated zest of 1 lemon
2 teaspoons fresh ginger, grated
6 sprigs rosemary
5 tablespoons good olive oil
salt & freshly ground black pepper

1   Heat the oven to 230°C/450°F/Gas Mark 8.

2   Mix together the parsley, thyme, garlic, lemon zest and ginger. Stuff this mixture into the cavity of the fish.

3   Oil a shallow ovenproof dish and line it with the rosemary. Lay the fish on top. Mix the olive oil with the lemon juice and pour over the fish.

4   Bake in the oven, uncovered, for 20-25 minutes, basting from time to time. Serve hot, accompanied by Salsa Verde (see page 12).

FISH COUSCOUS

On the Mediterranean coast of Africa couscous is more than a dish, it is a way of life. Couscous is a staple made from semolina coated with flour; when steamed those little grains are light and fluffy, the ideal medium for soaking the delicious gravy of soupy stews served with couscous. The stew can be made from practically anything: lamb, beef, game, poultry or fish. It should be cooked with plenty of vegetables and chickpeas making couscous a deliciously satisfying, well balanced and healthy meal.

Steaming couscous in the traditional way is a lengthy process. The following recipe, however, gives an easy and quick way for cooking it and, although the results are not quite as light and fluffy as the original, it does produce a very good alternative.

Serves 6-8

for the couscous
5 tablespoons good olive oil
500 g/1 lb/3 cups couscous
1 litre/2 pints/4 cups stock or water
1 scant teaspoon salt

for the stew
3 tablespoons light olive oil or groundnut oil
1 teaspoon ground coriander seeds
1/2 teaspoon whole cumin seeds
1/2 cinnamon quill or scant 1/2 teaspoon powdered cinnamon
8 shallots, peeled & quartered
4 cloves of garlic, peeled & quartered
3 courgettes, trimmed & sliced
1 fennel bulb, sliced
1 litre/2 pints/4 cups fish stock or 1/2 water and 1/2 dry white wine
a large pinch of saffron (optional)
salt
750 g/1 1/2 lb steaky white fish such as halibut, monkfish & cod, a mixture, sliced into large chunks
1 tablespoon coriander, roughly chopped

1/2 recipe harissa (see page 9) so each diner can have a taste

1   To make the couscous, heat the oil in a heavy bottomed pan. Add the couscous and fry for a minute or two or until the grains start to change colour. Add the liquid and the salt and bring to the boil. Reduce the heat to a minimum, cover the pot tightly and simmer, very gently, for 20 minutes. Switch off the heat and let the couscous rest for about 5 minutes. Fluff up with a fork.

2   To make the stew, heat the oil in a large, heavy bottomed pan. Add the spices and fry for a second or two. Add the vegetables and continue frying, mixing until all the ingredients are shining and nicely coated with the spice mixture. Add the stock, wine and saffron, and bring to the boil. Reduce the heat to a minimum and simmer very gently for 10-15 minutes. Add the fish and continue to simmer for 8-10 minutes or until the fish is just tender when tested with the tip of a knife.

3   In a large flat serving bowl, arrange a crown of couscous. Lay the cooked fish and vegetables in the centre and pour some of the cooking liquid over the fish. Decorate with fresh coriander or parsley leaves and serve together with the rest of the cooking liquid and the harissa.

STUFFED SARDINES AIDA

The name of the dish does not refer to the famous opera, but to Aida Lavagna, a vivacious and talented cook, larger than life and twice as much fun. Dressed to kill and adored with her permanent, exotic turban, she used to make these delicious little snacks to be eaten cold on the plaza. Sadly Aida is no longer with us, but her memory lives on in this wonderfully simple dish.

12 sardines, butterflied with head and central bone removed (ask the fishmonger to do this for you)
100 g/4 oz/½ cup ground almonds or bread crumbs
6 anchovy fillets, chopped
75 g/3 oz/⅓ cup cheese, grated (strong-flavoured Spanish, or Cheddar will do)
1 tablespoon capers, chopped
3 tablespoons parsley or dill, finely chopped
a few sprigs of marjoram, finely chopped
grated zest and juice of ½ lemon
1 egg
salt & freshly ground black pepper

1 Heat the oven to maximum (250°C/475°F/Gas Mark 9).

2 To butterfly the sardines, first scale and wash them. Remove the heads and split the fish open. Grab hold of the spinal bone and slide a small knife along the bone, lifting it and separating it clean from flesh.

3 Mix the ground almonds together with the chopped anchovies and half the cheese. Reserve the other half of the cheese. Add the rest of the ingredients and mix well.

4 Lay 6 sardines, skin down, on a chopping board. Top each with about a tablespoon of the stuffing and spread to an even layer. Sandwich with the remaining 6 sardines. Transfer the sardine pairs to a well oiled baking dish, brush with olive oil and sprinkle with the rest of the cheese. Bake on the top shelf of the hot oven for 10-12 minutes until the sardines are cooked and nicely browned. Serve with wedge of lemon, on a bed of lettuce, either hot or at room temperature. The stuffed sardines can also be grilled or barbecued.

STUFFED MACKEREL

The mackerel, like the tuna, is loved all over the Mediterranean. Indeed freshly caught mackerel plainly barbecued on the quayside, served with a sharp sauce such as Agro-Dolce (see page 16) or just lemon juice, is one of the great pleasures of the Mediterranean summer.

This is my interpretation of an old Hebrew recipe.

4-6 small mackerel, cleaned & as fresh as possible
3 tablespoons lemon juice
100 g/4 oz/½ cup dry white wine
small bunch of dill
salt & freshly ground black pepper
50 g/2 oz/¼ cup fish stock or water
500 g/1 lb/2 cups leeks with some of the green left on, washed, trimmed & sliced

1 Heat the oven to 220°C/425°F/Gas Mark 7.

2 Make 3 deep slashes on each side of the fish and sprinkle both outside and inside with the lemon juice and salt. Allow to marinate until the stuffing is ready.

3 Place the leeks and dill in a food processor and process, starting and stopping the machine, until roughly chopped. Season with salt and pepper.

4 Divide half of the leek mixture equally between the fish and stuff it into the cavity. Use the rest to line the bottom of a large, well greased, baking dish. Place the fish on the leek bed and pour the wine and stock over. Season and bake in the oven, uncovered, for about 15-20 minutes, turning the fish once and basting frequently. Serve either hot or cold accompanied by a salad such as celery and tomato (see page 48) or prawn and orange salad (see page 45) or Moroccan lemon salad (see p50).

LIBYAN FISH

This is a delicious and extremely easy way of cooking oily fish such as grey mullet or mackerel. Here it is served hot but it is also good served as a part of a cold buffet.

3 tablespoons olive oil
1 teaspoon whole cumin seeds
1 small head of garlic, peeled & chopped
1-2 green chillies, sliced (optional)
juice of 1 lemon
150 ml/6 fl.oz/³⁄4 cup fish stock or water
salt
1 kg/2 lb fish, cleaned & sliced into 6-8 portions
1 tablespoon capers, rinsed
a small bunch of flat-leaf parsley, leaves only

1   Heat the oil in a heavy bottomed frying pan, add the cumin and fry until the seeds start to pop and emit a pleasant, roasted smell.

2   Add the garlic and chillies if used and continue frying until the garlic starts to change colour. Add the lemon juice and stock, and bring to the boil. Reduce the heat and simmer for 5 minutes.

3   Add the fish, season with salt, cover and simmer for 15 minutes or until the fish is just done. Sprinkle with capers and parsley and serve, decorated with lemon wedges.

RED MULLET IN A PARCEL

Barbunya – or Sultan Ibrahim as it is known by the Arabs – is king of the Mediterranean fish. This small red relative of the Atlantic red mullet, with a golden stripe running along its body, is the embodiment of fishiness – it smells of sea and iodine and has an exquisite, white, flaky flesh. It is not surprisingly called the woodcock of the sea.

The best way to cook the fish is to dip it in seasoned flour and fry it crisply in boiling olive oil. In many countries the mullet is not gutted before cooking as the innards and especially the liver impart an intense gamey flavour.

The recipe below is almost as good. Mediterranean barbunya appears from time to time in many fishmongers and is well worth trying. If unobtainable use Atlantic red mullet.

6 pieces of silver foil measuring 20x20 cm/8x8 in
3 tablespoons olive oil
1 medium fennel, sliced across thinly
1 medium onion, sliced into thin rings
6 red mullets, scaled, cleaned & washed
a few sprigs of thyme
2 cloves of garlic, peeled & sliced thinly
6 thin slices of lemon
salt & freshly ground black pepper

1 Pre-heat the oven to 200°C/400°F/Gas Mark 6.

2 Oil the centre of each foil square generously (this will use roughly half the oil) and distribute the sliced fennel and onion evenly.

3 Stuff the cavity of each fish with a sprig of thyme and some garlic and lay them on top of the vegetables. Sprinkle with the rest of the oil. Lay a slice of lemon on each, season with salt and pepper and parcel up tightly. Bake them in the pre-heated oven for 10-15 minutes, opening the parcels for the last 5 minutes.

4 When the fish is nicely browned, serve decorated with lemon wedges. If more salt is needed, sprinkle with a bit of coarse sea salt.

DESSERTS

STUFFED FIGS

In my mind, figs are forever associated with sensual, cool, end-of-summer evenings. One of the first fruits cultivated by man, the magnificent fig tree still dominates the landscape of large parts of the Mediterranean, from Spain right round to Morroco.

Figs are best eaten simply. Peeled or unpeeled, they can be accompanied by a strongly flavoured cheese; or serve them as a first course stuffed with feta or any other salty goat or sheep's milk cheese flavoured with fresh chopped mint.

Select figs that are unblemished, very ripe and just firm to the touch. This dish is decorated with fresh bay leaves which, as well as providing a luscious green decoration, add their pungent smell.

250 g/8 oz/1 cup mascarpone, well chilled
75 g/3 oz/⅓ cup glacé mixed peel, finely chopped
1-2 tablespoons good honey
1 tablespoon grappa, marc or brandy
a few drops of orange blossom water
2-3 figs for each portion
bay leaves for decoration

1 Place all the ingredients with the exception of the figs into a mixing bowl and mix well.

2 Slice the figs across and across again, creating 4-petalled 'flowers' which are still joined at the stem end. Fill each of these with the cheese mixture. Decorate and chill for at least 2 hours before serving.

STUFFED DATES

This recipe was probably written down 1800 years ago, and is attributed to the legendary Roman food writer, Epicus. In the original, the stuffed figs were coated with salt and fried in honey to produce a rather strange flavour. Served here accompanied with cream as a tempting dessert or on their own as an interesting Christmas *petit-fours*, these dates are always appreciated!

150 g/6 oz/³⁄4 cup peeled pistachio nuts (reserve 1 nut for each date)
1-2 tablespoons fragrant honey
50 g/2 oz/¹⁄4 cup – 75 g/3 oz/¹⁄3 cup ground almonds
3-4 fresh dates per person, stones removed
2 teaspoons orange blossom or rose water

1   Place the pistachios and honey in a food processor and process at high speed until coarsely ground.

2   Transfer the content to a mixing bowl. Add the ground almonds and mix well. If the mixture is too loose add some more ground almonds.

3   Stuff a little of the mixture into each date, and decorate with a pistachio nut. Either arrange on individual serving plates on a pool of thick cream or serve in paper cases as *petit-fours*.

SCENTED PEARS

The inspiration for the following recipe is a classic Provençal dish which was quoted by Roger Vergé – a true Mediterranean whose food reflects the tradition and flavour of the region. In the original pears or peaches are flavoured with black pepper and bay leaves. One day I was short of fresh bay leaves and I used fresh lavender sprigs – another Mediterranean favourite – and it worked very well. If you do not have lavender growing in your garden, use 1-2 tablespoons dried lavender flowers instead.

This dish can be served hot but it is much better to let the pears cool in their cooking liquor and serve them at room temperature. For extra richness, thick cream could be served.

1 bottle full-bodied soft red wine
6 tablespoons lavender- or any other fragrant honey
2 tablespoons black peppercorns, tied in a muslin bag
6 sprigs of lavender flowers
juice and zest of 1 lemon
6 ripe pears, peeled with the stem attached
6 sprigs of lavender flower (optional) and mint to decorate

1 Combine the wine, honey, peppercorns, lavender flowers and lemon juice and zest in a large, heavy bottomed pan. Bring to the boil and cook for 2 minutes.

2 Reduce the heat, add the pears and simmer, very gently, for 10 minutes. Remove from the heat and allow to cool. Serve the pears with a little of the cooking liquid and decorated with the lavender blossom and mint.

ORANGE & ALMOND CUSTARD

This light and tasty custard comes from Spain and contains two of the most favourite Mediterranean ingredients - oranges and almonds.

The addition of orange blossom water (although not essential) gives this dish its characteristic perfume. It can be easily bought in any good Mediterranean or Middle Eastern store.

30 ml / 12 fl.oz / 1½ cups freshly squeezed orange juice
2-3 drops natural almond essence
1 tablespoon orange blossom water
6 egg yolks
100 g / 4 oz / ½ cup sugar
125 g / 5 oz / ⅔ cup ground almonds

1   Heat the oven to 180°C/350°F/Gas Mark 4.

2   In a small pan combine the orange juice, almond essence and orange blossom water. Bring to the boil and remove the pan from the heat.

3   In a mixer beat the yolks with the sugar for a minute or two until the mixture is pale and fluffy. Pour in the hot juice, add the ground almonds and mix well.

4   Divide the mixture between 6 small ramekins. Arrange the ramekins in a roasting pan and pour in boiling water to come halfway up the sides of the ramekins. Bake in the pre-heated oven for 20 minutes or until the custard is just set. Serve either hot or cold.

ALMOND CAKE WITH MANDARIN SYRUP

When winter sets in, the Mediterranean basin is literally awash with an amazing variety of citrus fruit. This pudding is wonderfully moist and fragrantly cake-like, making full use of the aromatic quality of those healthy, versatile fruits. Serve it either hot or cold accompanied by thick cream or, even better, with a large dollop of clotted cream.

150 g / 6 oz / 3/4 cup softened butter
75 g / 3 oz / 1/3 cup caster sugar
1 teaspoon grated orange peel
1 teaspoon grated lemon peel
3 eggs
150 g / 6 oz / 2/3 cup ground almonds
3 tablespoons plain flour
a few drops of natural bitter almond essence
2 teaspoons orange blossom water
butter for greasing
2-3 tablespoons ground almonds or breadcrumbs

for the syrup
100 g / 4 oz / 1/2 cup fresh mandarin or orange juice
1/2 teaspoon grated mandarin or orange peel
3 tablespoons good honey or sugar
2-3 tablespoons mandarin liqueur
mandarin segments for decoration

1   Heat the oven to 200°C/400°F/Gas Mark 6.

2   Place the softened butter and the sugar in the bowl of a food mixer and whisk at high speed for 3 minutes or until the butter is white and fluffy. Gradually add the rest of the ingredients and beat to a smooth cream.

3   Butter well a 23 cm/9 in flan dish, sprinkle with the ground almonds and knock out the excess. Pour the creamed mixture into the dish and spread it out evenly with a small spatula or the back of a spoon. Bake in the oven for 15-20 minutes or until set.

4   To make the syrup, combine the first three ingredients in a small sauce pan. Bring to the boil and simmer for about 5 minutes. Remove from the heat, cool slightly and add the liqueur. When the cake is cooked, pour the hot syrup over it, decorate with mandarin segments and serve from the flan dish, either hot or cold.

POMEGRANATES SERVED WITH CREAM

All around the Mediterranean the pomegranate is supposed to be a sacred fruit. In the Jewish tradition, it is said to have as many seeds as the number of good deeds the pious have to perform (start counting!). Crunching the seeds between your teeth is part of the fun of eating this exotic fruit.

The easiest way to peel a pomegranate is to remove its top and base, exposing the jewel-like red seed mass. Then, with a sharp knife, score through the outer peel so dividing the fruit into 4 segments. With your hands prise the peel from the delicate seeds, being careful to remove all traces of the thin yellow skin, which is very bitter. It sounds complicated but the whole process is rather quick and easy. It takes less than 5 minutes to prepare a fruit.

2 large pomegranates, prepared as above
500 g / 1 lb / 2 cups crème fraîche or Greek yogurt, well chilled
50 g / 2 oz / 1/4 cup granulated sugar
1 tablespoon orange blossom water or a few drops of vanilla extract
Grated zest of 1/2 lemon
25 g / 1 oz / 2 tablespoons flaked almonds
4 sprigs mint

1   Peel the pomegranates as described above.

2   Combine the crème fraîche or yogurt with the sugar, orange blossom water and the lemon zest, and mix well.

3   In each of 4 tall glasses arrange the pomegranate seed and cream mixture in alternate layers, finishing with cream. Sprinkle with almonds, decorate with a sprig of mint and serve.

DEMIRHINDI SERBETI

This recipe was given to me by Raphaela Lewis, one of the greatest authorities on everyday life in the Ottoman Empire. She tells a charming story about how the ice came to Istanbul from mountains situated hundreds of miles away: it was packed in thick felt cloth and first transported by a mule caravan, and then by sea until it finally arrived at the Sultan's table.

Now all you need for this surprisingly simple sorbet is a food processor and some ice cubes.

Make the sorbet immediately before serving. Other sweet syrups such as rose, mint or pomegranate cordial can also be used, in which case the addition of honey is unnecessary.

Serves 6

750 ml / 1½ pints / 4 cups ice cubes
a few drops of orange blossom water
4 tablespoons tamarind paste diluted with 100 ml / 4 fl. oz / ½ cup very cold water
4 tablespoons good runny honey
6 sprigs of mint

1 Put the ice into the food processor and process to a fine snow.

2 Divide the snow between 6 serving glasses and sprinkle with a few drops of orange blossom water.

3 Mix the tamarind paste with the honey. If it is too thick, dilute with a few drops of water. Pour this mixture over the snow, decorate with mint sprigs and serve immediately.

Index

Ahivetch, *55*
Almonds
    almond cake with mandarin syrup, *91*
    cold almond soup, *23*
Anchovies
    tapenade, *14*
    veal in anchovy & caper sauce, *62*
Apricot sauce, lamb steaks with, *57*
Artichoke salad, *47*
Aubergines
    aubergine & tomato salad, *49*
    aubergine soup, *21*
    deep fried aubergine, *43*
Avgolemono, *14*

Bread
    panzanella, *52*
Broad beans served with yogurt, *37*
Burgul pilav, *67*

Celery & tomato salad, *48*
Chard
    fried spinach salad, *54*
Cheese
    leek kuftadas, *32*
    spinach & feta cheese pie, *31*
    white foam soup, *29*
Chicken
    chicken breast cooked with peppers & sun dried tomatoes, *64*
    chicken cooked with olives & orange, *63*
    quick chicken stock, *19*
Chillies
    harissa, *9*
Couscous, fish, *77*
Cucumber
    salata de pipino, *45*
Cumin soup, *29*
Custard, orange & almond, *90*

Dates, stuffed, *86*
Demirhindi serbeti, *94*
Duck
    breast of Barbary duck in tamarind sauce, *71*

Eggs
    herb omelette, *33*
    Navatu eggs, *32*
    spring onion & tomato eggah, *34*
    tuna eggah, *36*

Figs, stuffed, *85*
Fish
    fish cooked in a spicy tomato sauce, *74*
    fish couscous, *77*
    fish stock, *17*
    grilled fish served with taramasalata, *74*
    Libyan fish, *81*
French beans
    cooked beans & tomato salad, *48*

Gaivetch, *55*
Garlic
    garlic sauce, *13*
    garlic soup, *28*

Harissa, *9*
Herb omelette, *33*
Honey
    demirhindi serbeti, *94*

Lamb
    barbecued shish kebabs, *58*
    coftas cooked in tahina sauce, *60*
    lamb coftas cooked with lemon & cumin, *61*
    lamb steaks with fresh apricot sauce, *57*
Leek kuftadas, *32*
Lemon
    avgolemono, *14*
    Moroccan lemon salad, *50*
Libyan fish, *81*
Liver
    chicken liver pilav, *66*
    lamb's liver with lemon & garlic, *41*

Mackerel, stuffed, *80*
Moroccan lemon salad, *50*
Mushroom & pancetta pasta, *68*
Mussel salad, *38*

Navatu eggs, *32*

Okra soup, *26*
Olives
    chicken cooked with olives & orange, *63*
    tapenade, *14*
Omelette, herb, *33*
Oranges
    almond cake with mandarin syrup, *91*
    orange & almond custard, *90*
    prawn & orange salad, *45*

Panzanella, *52*
Pasta
    mushroom & pancetta pasta, *68*
    pasta with spicy Italian sausages, *69*
Pears, scented, *89*
Peppers
    chicken breast cooked with sun dried tomatoes &, *64*
    tuna served with pepper & olive sauce, *73*
Pie, spinach & feta cheese, *31*
Pilav
    burgul, *67*
    chicken liver, *66*
Pomegranates served with cream, *92*
Prawns
    prawn & orange salad, *45*
    prawns in tomato & chilli sauce, *75*
Pumpkin & tomato soup, *24*

Red mullet in a parcel, *82*
Rice
    chicken liver pilav, *66*
Roes, smoked cod
    taramasalata, *40*

Salads
    ahivetch or gaivetch, *55*
    aubergine & tomato, *49*
    celery & tomato, *48*
    cooked beans & tomato, *48*
    fried spinach, *54*
    Moroccan lemon, *50*
    panzanella, *52*
    prawn & orange, *45*
    raw artichoke, *47*
    salata de pipino, *45*
    warm mussel, *38*
Salata de pipino, *45*
Salsa agro-dolce, *16*
Salsa verde, *12*
Sardines
    stuffed sardines Aida, *79*
Sauces
    avgolemono, *14*
    garlic, *13*
    harissa, *9*
    rough tomato, *10*
    salsa agrofdolce, *16*
    salsa verde, *12*
    spicy tomato, *11*
    tahina, *9*
    tapenade, *14*
Sausages, pasta with spicy Italian, *69*
Sea bass, baked, *75*
Sorbet
    demirhindi serbeti, *94*
Soups
    aubergine, *21*
    cold almond, *23*
    cumin, *29*
    garlic, *28*
    okra, *26*
    pumpkin & tomato, *24*
    white foam, *29*
    winter tomato, *24*
Spinach
    fried spinach salad, *54*
    spinach & feta cheese pie, *31*
Spring onion & tomato eggah, *34*
Stock
    fish, *17*
    quick chicken, *19*

Tahina sauce, *9*
    coftas cooked in, *60*
Tamarind paste
    breast of Barbary duck in tamarind sauce, *71*
    demirhindi serbeti, *94*
Tapenade, *14*
Taramasalata, *40*
    grilled fish served with, *74*
Tomatoes
    fish cooked in a spicy tomato sauce, *74*
    Navatu eggs, *32*
    prawns in tomato & chilli sauce, *75*
    rough tomato sauce, *10*
    spicy tomato sauce, *11*
    winter tomato soup, *24*
Tuna
    tuna eggah, *36*
    tuna served with pepper & olive sauce, *73*

Veal in anchovy & caper sauce, *62*

White foam soup, *29*

Yogurt, broad beans served with, *37*